THE EARLY HOMOSEXUAL RIGHTS MOVEMENT
(1864-1935)

John Lauritsen and David Thorstad

TIMES CHANGE PRESS
62 W. 14th ST., NEW YORK, NY 10011

Copyright © 1974 by John Lauritsen and David Thorstad

Printed in U.S.A.
First Printing

Times Change Press
62 W. 14th St., NY NY 10011

Library of Congress Cataloging in Publication Data

Lauritsen, John.
   The early homosexual rights movement (1864-1935)

  Bibliography: p.90; Index: p.92
  Gay liberation movement—History. I. Thorstad,
David, joint author. II. Title.
HQ76.5.L38   301.41'57'09   74-79104
ISBN 0-87810-527-1
ISBN 0-87810-027-X (pbk.)

. . . .

We would like to express special appreciation to Dr. Warren Johansson, Jonathan Katz, and Carol Lisker for their help in gathering and preparing some of the material in this book.

Logo from the German edition (1923) of Grigorii Batkis' The Sexual Revolution in Russia.

THE 100th ANNIVERSARY OF GAY LIBERATION

The June 1969 Stonewall riots in New York City are generally viewed as marking the beginning of the gay liberation movement. This view is based on a lack of information. In reality, the Stonewall riots represent not the beginning of gay liberation but the beginning of a *new wave* of gay liberation. 1969 marks a rebirth, an anniversary—indeed, one might say the 100th anniversary of gay liberation.

As in the women's movement, with the gay movement we are presently witnessing a kind of "second wave." And just as the history of the early wave of women's struggle needs to be rediscovered, so it is with the homosexual rights struggle. Unlike the history of the women's movement, however, the history of the first wave of gay liberation has been almost *entirely* suppressed and, thanks to the efforts of Stalinism and Nazism, many traces of it obliterated.

So effective has this suppression been that the mere assertion today that there *was* a gay liberation movement in the second half of the Nineteenth Century and the first three decades of the present one may at first arouse disbelief. Yet not only did such a movement exist, but it was a vital and growing movement that had a measurable impact on other social and political movements, not to mention literature and the arts.

The aim of this book will be to sketch briefly the history of this early struggle for homosexual rights, its rise and decline, and to discuss some of the issues it raised, with the hope that this will contribute to the gay liberation struggle today and to the revolutionary movement as a whole.

THE EARLY HOMOSEXUAL RIGHTS MOVEMENT
(1864-1935)

Beginnings of a Movement

Stonewall, we said, in a sense marks the 100th anniversary of the gay liberation struggle. In the late 1860s, a new penal code was proposed for Prussia that added homosexual acts (among males) to the category of crimes. In 1871, this provision was introduced by the Reichstag with no debate as Paragraph 175 of the new penal code for the Second Reich.

While the German legislators displayed a lightminded attitude in legalizing homosexual oppression, however, their move did not go unnoticed by homosexuals. In 1869, a Hungarian doctor by the name of Benkert (who used the pseudonym K.M. Kertbeny) wrote a lengthy open letter to the minister of justice, tracing the history of the rational approach to homosexuality, and arguing that the state has no business sticking its nose into people's bedrooms. He defended homosexual behavior with what might be called "gay pride," and called upon the authorities to reject the proposed paragraph.

Benkert was also the person who, in 1869, devised the term "homosexuality," which has come to be the generally accepted term for designating sexual acts between persons of the same sex.

Benkert's open letter reflected a defiance and indignation at bigotry, ignorance, and intolerance that one might easily associate with the militancy of the gay movement today. Since the French Revolution, he pointed out, reform was on the agenda and in the air. The reform trend was manifest in the laws on homosexuality, too. In the aftermath of the Napoleonic Code, which placed homosexuality on the same legal ground as heterosexuality, some German states, too, had begun to revise their penal codes, making homosexual acts legal. By the time of his letter, three states had done so, among them

6

Hannover, where the law had been drafted in 1840 by the present minister of justice.

By that time, however, other German states were independently beginning to strengthen their laws against homosexuality. Benkert saw in this trend both a threat to the freedom of gays and, with state-wide Paragraph 175, a danger signal that the clock of history might be turned backwards.

Even unrestrained freedom for gays, he argued, would pose no threat because homosexuality is inborn, not acquired. Heterosexuality (or what he called "normal sexualism") remains the stronger drive for the majority of the population. Straights, therefore, need not fear that freedom for gays would result in their proselytizing for a form of sexual expression that was by nature alien to heterosexuals.

This attempt to reassure straight society is a theme that was to be voiced often by gays in the first wave of the gay liberation movement. It was not so much an effort to make concessions to the potential wrath of an assumed heterosexual majority, but was mainly an attempt to lay the basis for launching an aggressive assault on the contradictions and hypocrisy of prevailing morality. If homosexuality is inborn, the argument went, it cannot be regarded as a punishable offense by rational persons who respect the mysterious laws of nature.

A society that proscribed homosexual love, Benkert pointed out, would place its historians in an awkward position. Dozens of the leading figures throughout history—including those of the Christian era—have been gay. Many of them were recognized as the "pride of our cultural history." Yet if the proposed penal code were adopted, such persons would have to be put in prison—a place of residence hardly suitable for persons acknowledged by all to have made important contributions to civilization.

Would imprisonment, Benkert asked, be an appropriate treatment for such royalty as Charles IX, Henry II, James I, Pope Julius II, Napoleon I, Louis XVIII, or Frederick the Great? Or for men of belles-lettres and science like Machiavelli, Michelangelo, Razzi ("Il Sodoma"), Shakespeare, Mazzarin, Molière, Newton, Winckelmann, Cambacérès, Byron, August Graf von Platen, and Eugène Sue?

The list mentioned only figures from the Christian era; but even with such a limitation, striking omissions are obvious. His argument could have been made even more compelling with the addition of others (and, indeed, he notes that thousands more would have to be included in any comprehensive listing of gays who have made important contributions to Western civilization and culture). Among them would be Bacon, Edward II, Sir Walter Raleigh, Marlowe, Hölderlin, Catherine the Great, Queen Kristina, Leonardo da Vinci, Cellini, and so on.

If such persons belong in jail, Benkert concluded, then "everything we have been taught about our history is nothing but lies and embellishment."

He concluded his open letter with a series of arguments intended to demonstrate that all scientific and practical knowledge about the nature of homosexual behavior rendered laws against it obsolete and anachronistic and placed a special obligation upon the "modern constitutional state" of the Nineteenth Century to help society "escape from the monstrous curse" of Judeo-Christian fanaticism that had claimed "millions of innocent victims." The state, he noted, has no business concerning itself with sex questions, provided the rights of others are not violated. Homosexuality not only does not violate those rights, but its presence in the sexual practices of all cultures, everywhere and at all times, is proof that it deserves recognition as a natural human phenomenon as much as heterosexuality. Besides, laws aimed at suppressing homosexual love are doomed to failure anyway: even the "most beastly persecutions" of the Judeo-Christian era have failed to eradicate it. Indeed, they could not help but fail because homosexuality is an "*inborn*, and therefore irrepressible, drive."

Benkert also put his finger on a key function of the persecution of homosexuals—that of creating social scapegoats for the majority. Innocent individuals are singled out for special disgrace and punishment by others, who often commit the same acts (though with persons of the opposite sex) but who can hold their heads high, secure in the knowledge that they will escape the vengeance of the law.

Benkert did not make his stand in a vacuum. For the 1860s saw the beginnings of what could be called scientific interest in homosexual behavior. And like the roots of the gay movement, the first efforts to develop a rational understanding of homosexuality can also be traced to Germany.

8

The largest body of literature on homosexuality in the 1860s was produced by Karl Heinrich Ulrichs, a German homosexual who knew Benkert. In 1864, he wrote his first "social and juridical studies on the riddle of love between men": *Vindex* and *Inclusa*. As early as 1862 he coined the term "Uranian" ("Urning" in German), based on the well-known myth in Plato's *Symposium*, to refer to homosexuals.* This term, widely used for decades both on the continent and in England, embodied the notion that homosexuals were a "third sex"—a woman's mind in a man's body, and *vice versa* for women. Mistaken though this notion was, both gays and straight supporters saw in it justification for their argument against persecuting people whose sexual orientation could be considered as inborn, "natural," and as unchangeable as that of the heterosexual male and female. (We will return to this matter later on.) Yet however antiquated Ulrichs' ideas may seem today, they were widely influential for decades and unquestionably represented a pioneering step a hundred years ago. He can quite properly be regarded as the grandfather of gay liberation.

The last two decades of the Nineteenth Century saw a proliferation of literary and scientific works dealing with homosexuality, especially in England (to which we shall return) and in Germany. Yet the promising beginnings of a movement to fight for homosexual rights, reflected in Benkert's open letter and in the efforts of Ulrichs, took approximately a quarter century to come to fruition, and, for the first time in history, to embark on the road of activism.

The Scientific Humanitarian Committee

In 1897, two years after Ulrichs' death, the first gay liberation organization was formed, in Germany. It was called the Scientific Humanitarian Committee. Its founder and guiding light throughout most of its thirty-five years of existence was Magnus Hirschfeld.

---

* In the *Symposium*, Pausanias refers to the goddess of men who love other men as the "Heavenly Aphrodite," and to homosexual love as "the beautiful love, the Heavenly love, the love belonging to the Heavenly 'Muse Urania.'"

Leaders of the Scientific Humanitarian Committee (composite photograph published in the July-October 1922 issue of the Yearbook). Left to right: Georg Plock; Dr. Ernst Burchard; Dr. Magnus Hirschfeld; Baron von Teschenberg.

The Committee published a Yearbook (*Jahrbuch für sexuelle Zwischenstufen*—Yearbook for Intermediate Sexual Types), which appeared more or less regularly (and for periods as a quarterly) between 1899 and 1923. This publication contained not only reports on the Committee's activities, but also literary, historical, anthropological, polemical, and scientific studies on the subject of homosexuality and other sex-related phenomena (such as transvestism). For a time the Committee also published a monthly report for its members, and it continued its publishing efforts—though sporadically toward the end—until 1933, when the rise of Nazism made further activity impossible.

In one of the early issues of its Yearbook, the Committee stated its goals as follows: (1) to win legislative bodies to the position of abolishing the antigay paragraph of the German penal code, Paragraph 175; (2) enlightening public opinion on homosexuality; (3) "interesting the homosexual himself in the struggle for his rights."

In line with these goals, it carried out various kinds of activities. It held regular public forums on homosexuality, it sent out representatives (Hirschfeld primarily) on speaking engagements and even international tours, it sent copies of its publications and other literature to governmental commissions studying revision of penal codes (in Russia and Switzerland, for example), and to public libraries, including the British Museum. The central, "activist" focus of the Committee, however, remained for more than two decades its petition campaign against Paragraph 175.

The Petition

The petition campaign was launched in 1897. Its aim was to collect as many signatures as possible of prominent political and artistic figures, scientists, and doctors, on a petition calling for the removal of homosexual acts from criminal status, except in cases involving the use of force, or arousing "public annoyance," or when performed between an adult and a minor under the age of 16.*

---

* Paragraph 175 of the German penal code still exists though it was modified in 1969—100 years after Benkert's open letter!—to remove homosexual acts

Supporters and proponents of the petition stressed several points in their efforts to expose the injustice of the antigay law: that since the Napoleonic Code was adopted in 1810, homosexual acts were legal in most countries in Europe, and that this had led to no ill side-effects for society; that the law punished sexual acts between two men but left unpunished the same acts when performed between a man and a woman or between two women; that it left millions of citizens prey to blackmailers and extortionists; that rather than deliver gays from their harmless and enjoyable penchant for same-sex relations, the law drove them to despair and frequently suicide.

The Committee gave top priority to its petition campaign. For years, the first article in its yearly and quarterly reports was frequently a detailed report on the current status of the struggle, with reprints from the press, correspondence, etc., indicating what response the Committee had received, and keeping its supporters up to date on the progress being made.

In its October 1910 issue, for instance, the Committee noted: "At present, the most timely and important question for the movement for homosexual liberation seems to us to be public opinion, and in particular the opinion of specialists, on Paragraph 250 (previously Paragraph 175) of the new draft penal code. Therefore, now as before, we shall orient our readers to all publications that take a stand either for or against the paragraph. The scope of material being published on this matter, however, is so great that we can only reproduce a few of the most typical examples."

---

between consenting adults from criminal status. In June 1973, the government further modified the law, but retained the provision outlawing homosexual acts between adults and minors (under the age of 18). German gays, however, are demanding complete repeal of the law, to make consenting homosexual sex legal irrespective of age. In doing so, they are not only continuing, but also going beyond, the struggle begun some seventy-five years earlier. It should be noted, incidentally, that in the ensuing years, the age of majority for homosexual acts has tended to increase, not only in Germany, but even in some countries like France, where the Napoleonic Code, which included no special law on homosexual acts, prevails. More recently, however (in Holland and Denmark, for instance), the trend seems to be toward lowering the age at which a citizen can legally decide to engage in homosexual acts to the early teens. The only proper formula, of course, is the *complete* removal of homosexual acts from the penal code, with punishment to be provided for only in cases involving the use of force.

While at times the petition campaign slackened—as it did, for instance, when the Committee struggled to defend itself during the antigay witch hunt of 1907 and also under the ravages of the first world war—it was never abandoned. Indeed, its most vigorous effort appears to have come after the war, when the Committee formed a united front in 1920 with two other gay groups—the German Friendship Association and the Community of the Special—to press forward the fight against the law.

From the very start the Committee won prominent supporters to the gay cause. On January 13, 1898, its first major supporter took the floor of the Reichstag to argue for the petition. He was the great Social-Democratic leader, August Bebel.

In addition to signing the petition, Bebel took copies of it into the Reichstag and urged his colleagues to add their names as well. Ridiculing the bourgeois government's approach to the matter, Bebel pointed out: "The number of these persons [gays] is so great and reaches so deeply into all social circles, from the lowest to the highest, that if the police dutifully did what they were supposed to, the Prussian state would immediately be obliged to build two new penitentiaries just to handle the number of violations against Paragraph 175 committed within the confines of Berlin alone."

At this point, the record of the proceedings indicates a commotion, with apparently a cry of protest from a certain von Levetzow. Bebel continued, "That is not an exaggeration, Herr von Levetzow; it concerns thousands of persons from all walks of life. . . . But gentlemen, let me say one thing. . . . If with regard to this law the Berlin police did their duty all the way, then there would be a scandal such as the world has never known, a scandal compared to which the Dreyfus scandal, the Lützow-Ledert and the Tausch-Normann-Schumann scandals are pure child's play."

Bebel's conception of the extensiveness of homosexual behavior was advanced for the period, half a century before the Kinsey investigations, and with anthropology only in its infancy. The Reichstag member who was shocked by Bebel's remarks was probably typical of most people then, in viewing homosexuality as a rare, mysterious, and unnatural phenomenon.

This, like a subsequent speech by Bebel on the petition campaign in 1907, was punctuated throughout by supporting shouts of "Hear! Hear!" from the Social-Democratic benches.

The Committee carried on a phenomenal amount of propaganda activity around its petition. In 1899, for instance, it sent a letter to Roman Catholic priests throughout the country requesting them to take a stand on the question of gay oppression and gay rights. In 1900, it sent copies of its Yearbook with the responses it had received, a pamphlet on the law, and a letter to all the members of the Reichstag and of the Federal Council. It also sent a letter to 2,017 daily newspapers; another to more than 8,000 top administrative officials, provincial councillors, mayors, and justice, police, and railroad officials; and yet another to public prosecutors and presidents of criminal courts throughout the entire Reich. The latter dealt in particular with a recent spate of convictions in the province of Hannover for homosexual acts, or, in legalese, "unnatural lewdness." In 1901, it sent 8,000 copies of the petition to judges. Ads were regularly placed in the press on behalf of its efforts.

The Committee also decided, in 1903, to publish "a generally understandable and convincing piece of propaganda that will make it possible to reach the broadest layers of the public with a refutation of the false conceptions that still often hold sway about the nature of Uranianism." Within four years this pamphlet, entitled *What the People Should Know About the Third Sex*, went into its nineteenth edition.

Support for the petition was not limited to a few isolated stars. More than 6,000 prominent figures signed it, of whom half were doctors. Some of the others were: Finance Minister Rudolf Hilferding, Hermann Hesse, Franz Werfel, George Grosz, Krafft-Ebing, Karl Kautsky, Eduard Bernstein, Lou Andreas-Salomé, Max Brod, Martin Buber, Albert Einstein, Käthe Kollwitz, Heinrich Mann, Thomas Mann, Carl Maria Weber, Stefan Zweig, Grete Meisel-Hess, Gerhardt Hauptmann, Karl Pauli, Rainer Maria Rilke, and Arthur Schnitzler.

In addition to German signers, the petition received the (unsolicited) backing of a number of outstanding international personalities, among them Zola, Tolstoy, the Danish critic Georg Brandes, and Norway's most prominent nineteenth-century poet, Bjoernstjerne Bjoernson, who sent Hirschfeld the following note in

December 1901: "For more than twenty years I have viewed this matter the same way you do, and if I were a German, I would sign."

Zola had been working on a novel called *Le Roman d'un inverti* (*The Novel of an Invert*), but he abandoned it because he was afraid to publish it. In a letter to a Dr. Laupts on the subject of homosexuality, published in the preface to the latter's book *Perversion et perversités sexuelles* (*Perversion and Sexual Perversities*), Zola observed that "anything that relates to sex relates to social life itself. An invert is a disorganizer of the family, of the nation, of humanity."

On October 18, 1907, more than 2,000 people attended a debate on Paragraph 175. The Committee later described the debate as "a high point of the movement, so to speak, which was soon to go into a sudden decline." The "decline" was brought on by the hysteria surrounding a series of trials involving homosexuality and prominent gays. The scandals lasted for several months and had a generally conservatizing effect on public opinion. (See footnote p.19.)

In late 1910 a new draft penal code was introduced that proposed to extend criminal status to include sexual acts between women. This move brought a new dimension to the struggle—the involvement of women's liberation groups.

By early 1911, meetings of women's organizations were being held throughout Germany to discuss ways to fight the proposed extension and to link the struggle of women with that of gays. A broad range of groups took up this matter, including Social-Democratic and bourgeois women's organizations.

One such meeting, reported at length in the Social-Democratic *Vorwärts*, was held in Berlin on February 10, 1911, by the local branch of the League for the Protection of Mothers. The turnout was so large that a second meeting had to be called two weeks later. The speaker for the Scientific Humanitarian Committee was Hirschfeld, who discussed the nature of homosexuality and the petition campaign.

Both meetings adopted a resolution condemning the law. This was the first public position taken by any important women's organization on this question. It called any attempt to extend criminal status to lesbianism "a serious mistake": "An inequality would not thereby be

15

eliminated, but rather an injustice doubled. The doors would be thrown wide open to informers and blackmailers, and unmarried working women who share living quarters with other women would be burdened in the most shamefully damaging way, without in the process any interest being protected. At a very minimum, the gathering regards it as absolutely necessary that medical experts— especially sex researchers and psychiatrists—as well as women, be consulted on this question."

Following the several-year-long dislocation caused by the first world war, the petition campaign, which had receded into the background, was aggressively resumed in order to fight yet another draft penal code (introduced in 1919), which, although it dropped any proposed extention of criminal status to lesbians, still provided for up to five years in jail for males who were convicted. Still, the more liberal climate prevailing in the period just following the war and the 1918 revolution gave gays considerable optimism that their struggle against the law was about to succeed.

In August 1920, the Committee held its first post-war general membership meeting. This meeting voted to form the united front of gay groups to fight the law, and it set up a special joint "action committee" to organize the fight. The committee was headed by Kurt Hiller.

In October 1921, a new minister of justice was appointed who was himself a signer of the petition.

Hopes were further buoyed when, after considerable pressure, the authorities agreed to provide a public hall *inside* the Reichstag building itself where the Committee could address interested members of the body. Fifty showed up for a speech by Hirschfeld on March 15, 1922.

The meeting, reported the Committee, was "a significant event in the history of our movement. We want to hope that it may serve to bring us a good distance closer to our goal in the struggle for liberation that we are engaged in."

On March 18, 1922, the signed petition was finally presented to the Reichstag—twenty-five years after it was launched. In December, the Reichstag voted to turn it over to the government for consideration. And there it appears to have remained, for, by 1923, the post-war economic and social chaos had reached such a point that the existence of the Committee began to be seriously threatened and the long efforts of the new gay movement that seemed so close to success were eclipsed.

The Role Played by Women

Although in Germany, as elsewhere, the legalized aspect of homosexual oppression touched male homosexuals more directly than

Rosa von Braunschweig (in drag). She wrote an article in Vol. 1 of the 1903 Yearbook on Felicita von Vestvali, an actress who played male roles.

females, the Scientific Humanitarian Committee made a conscious effort to attract lesbians. Its publications and forums provided a platform for lesbian feminists to educate on a number of questions, including the relationship between lesbian liberation and women's liberation in general.

Nevertheless, lesbians and lesbian feminism played a small role in the early movement. One obvious reason for this is the fact that the main focus of the early movement, opposition to antigay laws, was not one that could be immediately or directly related to homosexual women, since those laws applied only to men. Then, as now, lesbians by and large appear to have concentrated their energies in the broader women's movement.

"We had first begun, at the beginning of 1901, to interest intellectually outstanding Uranian ladies in our work," wrote Hirschfeld in May 1902. "They have subsequently become an almost indispensable and prominent component of all our events. Although the homosexual woman is not subject to any legal restrictions in Germany, she nevertheless suffers in the most varied ways because of the ignorance about her nature. The homosexual man and the homosexual woman are linked by a natural kinship with one another, and in fact belong to a third sex to which they are both equally entitled to lay claim, even though it does not affect them in the same way."

An example of the way in which the Committee attempted to link the gay struggle and the women's struggle occurred at an annual meeting of the Committee in the Hotel Prinz Albrecht in Berlin on October 8, 1904. The gathering heard a speech by lesbian feminist Anna Rühling on the topic "What Interest Does the Women's Movement Have in a Solution to the Homosexual Problem?" Although the title may not sound very militant, the speech certainly was. It leveled a blast at the women's liberation groups, in which lesbians were active, for not recognizing the important links between the oppression of women and the special oppression of lesbians. "When we consider all the gains that homosexual women have for decades achieved for the women's movement," she said, "it can only be regarded as astounding that the big and influential organizations of this movement have up to now not raised one finger to secure for their not insignificant number of Uranian members their just rights as far as the state and society are concerned, that they have done nothing—and I mean not a thing—to protect so many of their best known and most devoted pioneers from ridicule and scorn as they enlightened the broader public about the true nature of Uranianism."

The Community of the Special

Although the Scientific Humanitarian Committee was the most influential and prominent German gay group, there were others. Of these, perhaps the most significant was the Community of the Special. Founded in 1902 under the inspiration of Benedict Friedländer, its orientation was more along cultural lines than that of the Scientific Humanitarian Committee, and under Friedländer it openly disputed Hirschfeld's single-minded stress—which he continued to maintain even after Freud's contributions had become general knowledge, and in spite of mounting ethnological and anthropological evidence to the contrary—upon the notion that homosexuality was an inborn condition. While it supported the petition campaign against Paragraph 175, it did not consider it so important as the Hirschfeld group did. Its publication, "Der Eigene" (The Special), a periodical (after 1906 it appeared in book form) of "art and masculine culture," first appeared in 1896. Its publisher, Adolf Brand, was more than once the target of court suits for publishing "indecent" material, such as gay love poems, photographs, etc.

During the Moltke-Harden-Eulenberg affair in 1907*, Brand

---

* The Moltke-Harden-Eulenberg affair grew out of attacks on Kaiser Wilhelm II's friend and adviser Prince Philipp zu Eulenberg and Count Kuno von Moltke. The attacks were published in the weekly, *Die Zukunft* (The Future), by its editor, Maximilian Harden, near the end of 1906. Harden's thesis was that Eulenberg had put together a clique around the Kaiser that was up to political intrigues. The clique, he alleged, was tied together by mysticism and by sexual inclinations that were "repugnant to prevailing norms." Moltke challenged Harden to a duel, but the latter refused. Then, in May 1907, Moltke brought a civil suit against the editor (whose magazine had paradoxically been one of the first to call attention to gay oppression and to come out against Paragraph 175), which resulted in the press' whipping up a campaign of antihomosexual hysteria,

Benedict Friedländer.

published an article on Paragraph 175. (The article was reissued in May 1914 under the title "Paragraph 175," because "the incredible, long-established situation of insecurity created by the constitutional state still prevails.") He blasted the paragraph as "a real priests' paragraph," for it "permits the most base kind of meddling in people's private lives, reduces the state to the position of being a kind of jailer for morality snoopers, and represents—inasmuch as it protects no legal rights . . .—quite simply an incredible encroachment upon the freedom of the individual."

While noting that the affair had made a positive contribution by demonstrating that homosexuals exist at all levels of society, including positions of leadership, the main effect of the trials, as Brand saw it, was to expose the inability of the law to do what it was ostensibly intended to do, namely to "bring to justice" those who engage in homosexual acts, who, according to his estimate, numbered 1,000,000 in Germany. Rather, the main function of a law like Paragraph 175, in his view, was to keep the masses in terror and awe of the ruling powers. It was, therefore, a tool of "class justice," and needed to be combatted as such. "Accursed feudal society," Brand quoted an unnamed government official as observing after seeing the files of the Berlin police on persons suspected of being gay.

The Community of the Special's relations with Hirschfeld's committee were often rocky, particularly in 1907, when an important split in the Scientific Humanitarian Committee occurred, led by Friedländer. (More on this in Part III.)

---

hailing Harden as a "liberator of the Fatherland."

Although Eulenberg was the hapless victim of the attacks, their real target was the Kaiser himself. Harden went so far as to accuse Eulenberg of being homosexual, and, by implication, suggested that this fact alone was sufficient basis for discrediting the Kaiser. Accusations of "unnatural vice" followed fast and furious, fueled by a series of trials (the last did not end until June 1909).

Early in this affair, in 1907, Brand, the publisher of "Der Eigene," made the foolish mistake of writing an article entitled "Prince Bülow and the Abrogation of Paragrpah 175" in which he claimed that Chancellor von Bülow was himself a homosexual. This resulted in Brand's being sued, by Bülow; in a parallel trial, Brand was found guilty and sentenced in November the same year to 1½ years in prison.

Differences of strategy among German gay groups prevented any united struggle against the antigay hysteria that accompanied this whole unfortunate affair.

Progress and Projects

By 1905, the Scientific Humanitarian Committee felt that it had succeeded in accomplishing an essential preliminary goal for gay liberation—making the "love that dare not speak its name" into a subject that was being widely talked about. "One thing has been achieved, and it is not the least important thing. The period of passing the matter over in silence and disregarding it is past, for good. We now find ourselves in the midst of a period of discussion. The homosexual question has become a genuine question, one which has given rise to lively debate, and which will continue to be discussed until it has been resolved in a satisfactory way."

By 1905, no sizable newspaper was able to ignore the question of the struggle against gay oppression. (The Committee's optimism proved excessive, however, and by the 1930s the "homosexual question" was to again be relegated to oblivion for several decades.) By June 1908, more than 5,000 gays had been in contact with or members of the Committee. In addition to the petition campaign, the Committee was involved in a number of projects and raised the question of gay rights in various ways.

Like the gay movement today, it confronted candidates during election periods, demanding that they take a stand on gay rights and on the petition. In the 1907 Reichstag election campaign, it received twenty responses to its questionnaire in this connection. By the 1912 campaign, ninety-seven candidates responded—only six of whom opposed gay rights. Of the ninety-seven, thirty-seven were elected (twenty-four of these were Social Democrats, who, as usual, made up the largest bloc of supporters of gay rights).

Shortly before the 1912 elections, a small, black-bordered ad appeared in several German papers. It went as follows:

"REICHSTAG ELECTION! 3rd Sex! Consider this! In the Reichstag on May 31, 1905, members of the Center, the Conservatives, and the Economic Alliance spoke *against* you; but *for* you, the orators of the *Left*! Agitate and vote accordingly!"

Rumors were not uncommon at the time—both among gays and in the bourgeois press—that in races where the vote was close, it was the gay vote that made the difference.

In 1903, Hirschfeld undertook what were undoubtedly the first large-scale statistical inquiries into homosexual behavior—an approach that pointed the way to the more comprehensive taxonomic investigations of Alfred Kinsey nearly a half century later. The studies—rather primitive and of dubious scientific value—were based on inquiries first sent to 3,000 students in Charlottenburg, and then 5,721 metal workers. The publication of the results prompted a Protestant pastor to press charges against Hirschfeld for "disseminating indecent writings" and "insulting" six student co-plaintiffs by publishing the report. Hirschfeld's defense lawyer thought it significant that not one of the more than 5,000 metal workers had objected to the questionnaire. Hirschfeld himself made a stirring speech in court defending the right of scientific investigation into homosexual behavior and the fight against ignorance and oppression.

"I would feel," he stated, "that I had brought down blame upon myself were I, who possess the knowledge that I have accumulated in the field of homosexuality, not to do everything in my power to destroy an erroneous idea, the consequences of which human language is not rich enough to describe. At the beginning of this very week, a well-known homosexual student at the School of Technology poisoned himself because of his homosexuality. In my medical practice, I have at present a student in the same school who shot himself in the heart. Just a few weeks ago, in this very room, I attended a case against two blackmailers who had driven a homosexual gentleman—one of the most honorable men whom I knew—to suicide—something a second individual, pursued by the same blackmailers, could only with difficulty be dissuaded from doing. I could present hundreds of cases like this, and others similar to it. I felt it was necessary to bring about this inquiry in order to free humanity of a blemish that it will some day think back on with the deepest sense of shame. Per scientiam ad justitiam!"

The court found that although Hirschfeld had not published anything "indecent," he had nevertheless run the "risk" of leading young, impressionable (and, to the court's way of thinking, heterosexual) young men down the path of "perverse tendencies" by merely raising the idea of homosexuality with them! In spite of the foolishness of the notion that the young needed a questionnaire on

Baron von Teschenberg (in drag), a leader of the Scientific Humanitarian Committee (see p.10).

"Being thoroughly convinced of the justice and importance of your endeavors, not out of vanity or other self-centered motives, I send you this picture, which reveals my true nature, gladly putting it at your disposal for publication along with my name in the Yearbook."

Baron Hermann von Teschenberg

the subject to get the idea that they could engage in homosexual acts, the court went on to fine Hirschfeld 200 Marks. The Committee, nevertheless, described this as a "significant moral victory."

The trial received a great deal of sympathetic newspaper coverage—including the German-language press in Brazil and Argentina—and Hirschfeld won considerable support from various organizations. The Social-Democratic *Vorwärts* went so far as to compare his persecution to Galileo's under the Roman Inquisition.

Another project in which the Committee participated was the first gay liberation film, "Anders als die Andern" ("Different from Other People"). It was produced by a brother by the name of Richard Oswald with the help of Hirschfeld. Shown to the press for the first time on May 24, 1919, it was banned from public showings by the government in August 1920. To our knowledge, no copies of this historic document have survived.

Like the gay movement today, the Committee also appealed to prominent personalities to "come out" and lend their prestige to the gay rights cause. Following the death of the Danish poet Herman Bang in January 1912, for instance, the Committee hinted strongly that he may have left behind some document that would take up the question of his homosexuality and urged other gay writers to do the same. "It is to be hoped that Herman Bang, who had an enthusiastic interest for our movement, spoke out even more clearly about the emotional side of his life in some manuscript that he may have left behind and that will hopefully not be withheld from the public. It is probably also finally time for homosexual poets and artists to freely and openly express themselves with regard to the emotional side of their own sexual feelings, for indeed they are especially equipped to use their works to bring an understanding of this kind of feeling to the masses."

Bang had indeed written such a document in which he "came out" posthumously. And the Committee's fears were well-founded, for Bang's executor and publisher, Peter Nansen, refused to allow the work to be published. His reason was that if the document were to see the light of day it would bring "monstrous harm to Bang's name." Even in death, Bang was denied the right to explain his view of the nature of homosexuality.

World War I dealt a severe blow to the Committee's efforts. Several hundred of its members, and thousands of its supporters, left for the front. Although it continued to hold meetings, its base of support tended to dissipate, and the general mood among the public was not conducive to advancing the cause of gay rights.

The Committee itself, though politically independent, appears to have taken a rather social-patriotic attitude toward the war. It combined social-patriotic references to the German cause with earnest expressions of its desire for peace and "active love for those of our brothers who are out there in the field." Many of the early fighters for gay liberation died on the imperialist battlefield.

Despite the prevailing social patriotism, the Committee did not strike off its list its members in "enemy" countries like England. Indeed, it continued to publish articles by them during the war and to remind its readers of the need for solidarity among gays.

Its foremost goal during the war was to keep the gay rights struggle alive so that it could blossom again once the hostilities had ceased. In its April 1915 issue it wrote: "We must be, and are, of course, prepared for any eventuality. What is necessary, however, is that the Committee be able to hold out and be there when—after what is hoped will be a quick, victorious end of the war—domestic efforts for reform are again stirred to activity, and when, therefore, the struggle for the liberation of homosexuals, too, picks up again."

The German revolution of November 1918 gave the gay movement renewed hope. From the very outbreak of the revolution, the Committee cast its lot with the new republic. In the new era of freedom and enlightenment that it foresaw emerging with the overthrow of the monarchy and militarism, it expressed the "firm hope that our movement, too, which is based on scientific research, will once again be able to move into the forefront and lead the struggle for homosexual liberation to its long-desired end."

"We took the most active part in all the revolutionary events," the Committee reported. One example of this was the speech by Hirschfeld to a mass meeting in Berlin during the height of the revolution on November 10. The meeting, in front of the Reichstag building, was called by the Bund Neues Vaterland (New Fatherland League), one of the first groups to actively support the rebellion. Between 3,000 and 4,000 people attended the rally. As bullets flew overhead and Red Guards attacked supporters of the Kaiser nearby, the well-known gay leader exhorted the crowd. In conclusion, he said:

"In addition to a true people's state with a genuinely democratic structure, we want a *social* republic. Socialism means: solidarity, community, mutuality, further development of society into a unified body of people. *Each for all and all for each*! And yet a third thing we want: The community of peoples, struggle against racism and national chauvinism, removal of limitations on economic and personal communication between peoples, the right of peoples to self-determination regarding their relationship to a state and their form of government. We want people's courts and a world parliament. In the future it should no longer be 'Proletarians,' but 'People of the World, Unite!' Before our eyes pass the great pioneers of the Social Democracy who are no longer in a position to experience this day: Ferdinand Lassalle, Karl Marx and Friedrich Engels, August Bebel, Wilhelm Liebknecht, and Paul Singer, and with them socialists from other countries, above all our French friend Jaurès. His death at the beginning of the world war shows that not only in Germany but elsewhere too nationalism attempted to destroy internationalism, and militarism attempted to destroy socialism. Citizens! Let us trust in the new republican government; let each person help to keep calm and order. Then we will soon be able to again lead a life of human dignity."

The Committee immediately sent a delegation to the new government to press for a total amnesty that would include the release from jail of all inmates convicted of homosexual acts. The removal of censorship and the greater freedom of the press and speech that ensued following the revolution were a boon to the gay rights struggle for a time. But perhaps the most tangible benefit to the gay movement was the acquisition of a building that was to become an international center for gay liberation and sex research.

The Institute for Sexual Science

The institute was housed in a lovely building that had belonged to Prince Hatzfeld prior to the revolution. It was one of the finest

27

palaces in Berlin. Hirschfeld purchased it with his own money and endowed it with his considerable collection of scientific material.

In his speech to the scholars, doctors, and politicians who attended the opening in July 1919, Hirschfeld called it "a child of the revolution"—not only of the uprising that swept Berlin on November 9, 1918, but also of the "great spiritual revolution" that had begun decades earlier with the first stirrings of the homosexual rights movement.

The Institute for Sexual Science was a repository for all kinds of biological, anthropological, statistical, and ethnological data and documentation relating to sexology. It became a kind of university for sex science, with regular classes on a variety of relevant subjects. It was the first institute of its kind anywhere in the world. It was truly a forerunner of the Kinsey Institute for Sex Research.

The Scientific Humanitarian Committee, while remaining organizationally independent of the Institute, set up offices in two rooms on the second floor. The building thus became an international center not only for sexual science but for the gay liberation movement.

Medical advice at the Institute was free and lectures by the Institute's specialists were open to the public. In 1919, a marriage counseling bureau was also opened at the Institute. It was consulted by thousands of people, and was so successful that it served as a pattern for similar endeavors in many other countries.

The procession of scientists and politicians who visited the Institute was long and numerous. Scores of persons at a time, representing various political groups, including a number of socialist youth groups and parties, would seek it out as a way of informing themselves on the subject of homosexuality and related questions. Every German who crossed its threshold was given an opportunity to sign the petition against Paragraph 175.

One such delegation to visit the Institute arrived on January 21, 1923. It consisted of Russian doctors, and was headed by the people's commissar of health. Here is what the Committee had to say about their visit in the 1923 issue of its Yearbook:

"On January 21, 1923, the film 'Anders als die Andern' was shown to the Russian doctors after they especially requested it. After seeing it, these gentlemen expressed their surprise that a film of such serious and decent content should arouse any scandal at all and that it could be banned. The Herr Minister of Health in conclusion stated how pleased he was that in the *new* Russia, *the former penalty against homosexuals has been completely abolished.* He also explained that *no unhappy consequences of any kind whatsoever have resulted from the elimination of the offending paragraph, nor has the wish that the penalty in question be reintroduced been raised in any quarter*."(The tsarist antihomosexual law was abolished by decree in December 1917. A decade after this visit by the people's commissar of health, Stalin reintroduced it.)

For fourteen years the Institute's unique collection of exhibits, its research work, its archives, and its library won for it an international reputation that attracted many foreign scientists and writers. Its brief life came to an abrupt end with the rise of Nazism.

Per Scientiam ad Justitiam

The Scientific Humanitarian Committee, whose motto was "per scientiam ad justitiam" (justice through science), played a role in stressing the need for scientific enlightenment and a rational approach to homosexuality and sexuality in general that went beyond its publications and the Institute to include direct participation in scientific gatherings. For instance, Hirschfeld was one of the speakers at the International Medical Congress in London, August 6-12, 1913. His participation at the gathering, attended by some 2,000 doctors from all over the world, was described by the Committee as "a success for our cause." While in London, he combined his scientific work with political activism by meeting with British gays to form a London branch of the Scientific Humanitarian Committee.

The Committee also organized an active intervention into the September 16-24, 1922, centennial gathering of German scientists and doctors in Leipzig, attended by more than 8,000.

Hirschfeld also played the key role in calling and helping to organize the first congress, in Berlin, of the World League for Sexual Reform in 1921. The Committee sought to insure that the oppression of homosexuals be recognized as a valid and significant question during the deliberations.

Uranians of the World, Unite!

The revival of the gay liberation struggle after the war was reflected in other ways as well. With the end of the war, the German gay movement sought to reestablish links with gay groups in other countries, especially England, where gays were most active. And at its first post-war general membership meeting August 28-30, 1920, the Scientific Humanitarian Committee passed a motion to this effect, in addition to setting up the united front with other gay groups to fight the antigay law. By the end of the war, the idea of forming a world gay organization was being tossed around. One reflection of this was the August 14, 1920, issue of the Community of the Special's publication, which contained an article entitled "Uranians of the World Unite!"

An example of this international outreach was the international speaking tours that Hirschfeld went on in the early twenties. In early 1922, he went on such a tour through Holland. The turnout at most of his meetings shows the widespread interest that prevailed in sexuality and the homosexual rights struggle. On his Dutch tour, he drew a full house in Amsterdam's Konzert-Gebouw and more than 900 in The Hague.

On May 25, 1922, he spoke in a concert hall in Vienna that seated more than 2,000. Only a few notices in the newspapers packed the hall and hundreds had to be turned away. He gave a three-hour speech. Five days later, he addressed a meeting in Prague at the invitation of the group "Urania." So many people showed up that seats had to be set up behind the film screen. He also addressed meetings in Italy.

With the post-war upturn in the gay rights movement came an increase in gay publications, and in 1921, the formation of a gay theater in Berlin, Eros Theater, where original gay plays were performed.

With the formation of the gay united front, the fight against the antigay paragraph also picked up. Besides stepping up the petition campaign, protest meetings were organized; one in Berlin in early 1921 drew more than 400 people.

In January 1921, the Action Committee of the united front issued an appeal "to the homosexuals of Germany" to join the struggle for gay rights. In it, it stated, among other things:

"Homosexuals, you know what the reasons and motives of your opponents amount to; you know, too, that your leaders and advisers have for decades been tirelessly working to destroy prejudices, spread truth, and achieve justice for you (and these efforts have certainly not been entirely without success); but in the last analysis, you must carry on the fight yourselves. In the final analysis, justice for you will be the fruit only of your own efforts. The liberation of homosexuals can only be the work of homosexuals themselves."

By the twenty-fifth anniversary in 1922, the Scientific Humanitarian Committee had about twenty-five branches throughout Germany.

The obviously successful post-war activities did not all occur without incident, however. For the ugly head of fascism and anti-Semitism reared itself early. On October 4, 1920, a meeting Hirschfeld was addressing in Munich was physically attacked, with the police dragging their feet on doing anything about it. In 1921, he was attacked by anti-Semites in Munich and left in the street for dead; his skull had been fractured.

One of the most vicious assaults came at a lecture in Vienna on February 4, 1923. This meeting was disrupted by Nazi youth who first hurled stink bombs and then opened fire, wounding a large number of members of the audience. Hirschfeld himself was not hurt.

In addition to working with other German gay and women's groups, the Scientific Humanitarian Committee maintained close ties with a number of foreign gay groups (which we shall take up shortly). Its outlook was consistently internationalist. An example of this was its top policy-making body, which, with a reorganization in 1906, consisted of twenty-eight members from Germany, Austria, Switzerland, Holland, Denmark, England, Italy, and Belgium.

The Gay Movement in England

Homosexual acts between adult men remained punishable by death in England until 1861 (and punishable by imprisonment until 1967).

Although the modification of the law was not the result of any campaign, nor did it give rise to the formation of a gay movement, the closing decades of the Nineteenth Century saw a phenomenal growth of a gay literary underground, or semi-underground (thoroughly documented in Brian Reade's book, *Sexual Heretics*, published by Coward-McCann in 1970). While Reade's assertion that "an increase in homosexuality was observable in England from about the middle of the nineteenth century onward" seems at best debatable, it is true that a great many prominent gay writers began to seriously come to grips with the question. (This trend, observable throughout Europe, received its first literary impetus from the Romantic period, with its rediscovery and glorification of Greek antiquity and the often homoerotic overtones of its cultivation of the ancient ethos.)

While it is not our purpose here to trace the rise of this gay literary phenomenon in the Victorian and post-Victorian periods, the nature of the gay liberation movement in England cannot be understood without some awareness of it.

One of the most pervasive influences on British gays in the second half of the Nineteenth Century was Walt Whitman. The publication of his *Leaves of Grass* in 1855, and particularly its highly homoerotic "Calamus" section, established him as the most influential of the poets who made homoerotic themes a prominent part of their writing. The unabashed joy of homosexual love that permeated his writing and his philosophy stirred gays throughout Europe for decades to a new pride in their homosexuality.

Among these was Edward Carpenter, a socialist, who, when the gay pantheon is filled, will certainly occupy a prominent position. Carpenter, a prolific writer, grappled with many subjects, among them homosexuality among primitive peoples, the constraining effects of "civilisation" and "commercialism," prison reform, the labor movement, Marx's labor theory of value, women's oppression and liberation, Oriental philosophy, and many other topics.

Carpenter visited Whitman twice, and wrote a book of poetry entitled *Towards Democracy*, published in 1883, that was inspired by Whitman's style and his vision of "comradeship." In an introductory note, Carpenter observed that *Towards Democracy* was to Whitman's *Leaves of Grass* as "the moon compared with the sun." It had a "milder radiance" that allowed one "to glimpse the stars behind. Tender and meditative, less resolute and altogether less massive, it has the quality of the fluid and yielding air rather than of the solid and uncompromising earth."

The book foresaw a socialist revolution that would inaugurate a new era of "democracy," "comradeship," and sexual freedom; his vision of the new society awarded a special role to homosexuals (who, in keeping with the times, he viewed as a "third sex" or "intermediate sex") in introducing humanity to this new era.

In 1894, Carpenter gave a public lecture in Manchester on "homogenic love"—a thing unimaginable until it was done. The speech was published in January 1895 by the Manchester Labour Press. The fourth of his pamphlets on sex to be published by the Labour Press (the others had sold well), this one caused some alarm.

In 1895, he began collecting material for a book entitled *Love's Coming-of-Age*. Then, in April, came the arrest of Oscar Wilde; the subsequent trials and antihomosexual hysteria dealt a serious blow to the developing British gay movement that lasted for at least a decade. In his autobiography, Carpenter wrote that from the moment of Wilde's arrest "a sheer panic prevailed over *all* questions of sex, and especially of course questions of the Intermediate Sex." Trains were reportedly filled with homosexuals rushing to flee England for the continent.

Following Wilde's arrest, Carpenter's publisher canceled his contract for *Love's Coming-of-Age* (although part of it had already been set) and refused to publish further editions of *Towards Democracy*. A half dozen other publishers also refused to touch *Love's Coming-of-Age*. "The Wilde trial had done its work; and silence must henceforth reign on sex-subjects," Carpenter wrote. His only hope of seeing his work published was the Manchester Labour Press, which brought both it and *Towards Democracy* out in 1896. "My book circulated almost immediately to some extent in the Socialistic world, where my name was fairly well known; but some time elapsed before it penetrated into more literary and more 'respectable' circles."

The book, which eloquently describes the oppression of women and hails the developing movement for women's rights, in addition to discussing homosexuality, was translated into a number of languages.

33

Carpenter wrote that at the first German Women's Congress in Berlin in 1912, the book "curiously enough became a sort of bone of contention, dividing the advanced party who took it as their text-book, from the more conservative party who anathematized it." By World War I, it had sold 50,000 copies. Besides German, Carpenter's books were translated into Italian, Bulgarian, Japanese, Norwegian, Dutch, Russian, and Spanish.

In addition to Carpenter, mention should be made of the contribution of John Addington Symonds to early gay literature. In 1883, he privately and anonymously printed an essay called "A Problem in Greek Ethics, Being an Inquiry into the Phenomenon of Sexual Inversion." This was the first serious study of homosexuality in English. He went on to play a large role in helping Havelock Ellis write his monumental *Studies in the Psychology of Sex*, published in 1897—in German, so as to avoid English censorship. Symonds' family bought up most of the edition and destroyed it; they insisted that his name be removed from forthcoming editions (he had died in 1893), and Ellis complied.

In 1914, Ellis and Carpenter founded the British Society for the Study of Sex Psychology. This group, which had 234 members in July 1920, concentrated on propagandistic and educational activities. It created a special gay subcommittee. Its pamphlets included an abridged version of the Scientific Humanitarian Committee's *What the People Should Know About the Third Sex.*

The abridged version, published in 1923 under the title *The Problem of Sexual Inversion*, stated in its introduction that the aim of the pamphlet was primarily "discussion and elucidation of the subject." The group felt that the German gay movement's focus on elimination of the antihomosexual law was not yet a feasible one for the British gay movement. ("We do not think the time has yet arrived in England for a similar demand to be made.") Instead, the Society appealed to straights to put themselves in the position of homosexuals, unjustly persecuted by prevailing heterosexual norms for a physical condition (as members of the "third sex") for which they could not reasonably be held accountable:

"Every normal being should try to imagine himself in the position of a uranian, a difficult but not an unprofitable task. His inner life resembles that of a man unjustly condemned, a man who does penance for a crime that he has not committed; he knows that he is guiltless of his own desires, that nature has played a trick on him and that, try as he may, he cannot think or feel except as she has ordered. This unhappy plight, which he has had no hand in bringing about, is the cause of contempt and loathing in the minds of those of his fellow-men who fail to grasp that his nature is not theirs." It emphasized that the "uranian" not only has a duty to accept his or her true nature, but can also make (and has made) a positive contribution to society. In view of this, society's persecution of homosexuals is something that works against its own best interests.

The British group founded a library and established a number of contacts in the United States, most important of whom was Margaret Sanger. With her aid, it announced plans to form an American branch in the early twenties.

If the approach of the Society seems a bit cautious, it might help to keep in mind the repressive circumstances in which it was forced to operate. Bertrand Russell, a delegate to the 1929 International Congress of the World League for Sexual Reform, held in London, described the difficulties imposed on British homosexual rights advocates by the prevailing censorship and obscenity laws:

"The condemnation of the *Well of Loneliness* [a lesbian novel by Radclyffe Hall] has brought into prominence another aspect of the censorship, namely, that any treatment of homosexuality in fiction is illegal in England. There exists a vast mass of knowledge on homosexuality obtained by students in continental countries where the law is less obscurantist, but this knowledge is not allowed to be disseminated in England either in a learned form or in the form of imaginative fiction. Homosexuality between men, though not between women, is illegal in England, and it would be very difficult to present any argument for a change of the law in this respect which would not itself be illegal on the ground of obscenity. And yet every person who has taken the trouble to study the subject knows that this law is the effect of a barbarous and ignorant superstition in favour of which no rational argument of any sort or kind can be advanced."*

---

* Publisher's note: American gay liberation literature is *currently* banned in England, shipments thereof being seized and destroyed by British Customs.

35

The Gay Movement in the United States and Other Countries

While the early gay movement developed most fully in Germany and England, and while its impact reached far beyond those places where actual gay groups became organized, brief mention should nevertheless be made of a few additional manifestations of the first wave of the homosexual rights struggle.

There does not appear to have been much, if any, organized gay rights activity in the United States during the period covered in this book. That does not mean, however, that the question of gay oppression and gay rights was in a state of complete limbo. In 1908, for instance, a work was privately published by an author who took the pseudonym Xavier Mayne entitled *The Intersexes: A History of Similisexualism as a Problem in Social Life.*

Mayne (whose real name was Edward I. Stevenson) had to go to Italy to get the book published. In the United States, he explained, some literature on homosexuality emanating from Germany was circulating at the time, but "hazardously and sparsely; and not with any real currency in social life. Even in order to own works of a medico-psychiatric sort, as the 'Psychopathia Sexualis' of Dr. von Krafft-Ebing, or Dr. Moll's 'Conträre Sexualität,' or Dr. Hirschfeld's studies, the volumes must be procured strictly on a physician's certificate!" With such restrictions on the dissemination of literature relevant to gay liberation, it is not surprising that there was no visible movement campaigning for gay rights on this side of the Atlantic.

This was not because homosexuality was not widespread in the United States, of course: ". . . of the enormous diffusion of Uranianism and of similisexual intercourse in the United States of America and in Canada, no possible doubt can exist, if the intelligent observer has resided there and has moved about in various social grades and circles of the larger cities." As "homosexual capitals" of his day, Mayne listed New York, Boston, Washington, Chicago, St. Louis, San Francisco, Milwaukee, New Orleans, and Philadelphia. An impressive list even today.

One of the first public supporters of gay rights in the United States was Emma Goldman. In the introduction to a lengthy article by her on Louise Michel published in the 1923 issue of the Scientific

36

Humanitarian Committee's Yearbook, Hirschfeld praised her for speaking up for the rights of those without rights, in her "Mother Earth" publication and in speeches all across the United States. "And so it is," Hirschfeld wrote, "that she became the first and only woman, indeed one could say the first and only human being, of importance in America to carry the issue of homosexual love to the broadest layers of the public."

In her article, Emma Goldman had the following observations on the question of gay rights:

"I regard it as a tragedy that people of a differing sexual orientation find themselves proscribed in a world that has so little understanding for homosexuals and that displays such gross indifference for sexual gradations and variations and the great significance they have for living. It is completely foreign to me to wish to regard such people as less valuable, less moral, or incapable of noble sentiments and behavior."

And: "Even years ago, when I still knew nothing about sex psychology and my only familiarity with homosexuals was limited to a few women whom I got to know in jail, where I wound up because of my political convictions, I firmly stood up in defense of Oscar Wilde. As an anarchist, my place has always been alongside the persecuted. The entire trial and conviction of Wilde struck me as *an act of horrible injustice* and repulsive hypocrisy on the part of the society that had condemned this man. And this alone was the reason for which I stood up for him.

"Later I came to Europe, where I found out about the works of Havelock Ellis, Krafft-Ebing, Carpenter, and many others, who introduced me to a full awareness for the first time of the crime committed at the time by Oscar Wilde and people like him. From that point on, I stood up both in my speeches and my writings for those whose sexual feelings and needs are differently oriented. Above all, it was your work, my dear doctor [Hirschfeld], that helped me to shed light on the extremely complicated problems of sex psychology and to develop a more human attitude toward this question among my audiences."

In Holland, following the adoption of the Dutch anti-homosexual paragraph on June 15, 1911, a Dutch branch of the Scientific

Humanitarian Committee was formed. This was the first of what was to become a series of foreign branches. It described its task as follows: "To spread enlightenment about the homosexual question in all layers of the Dutch population and to demand the same rights for homosexuals as exist for heterosexuals, and above all the same estimation and treatment." It immediately got thirty prominent figures to sign an appeal to this effect. It also published a Dutch version of the pamphlet *What the People Should Know About the Third Sex*.

By early 1914, a branch of the Scientific Humanitarian Committee had been formed in Austria, in Vienna, and was holding public lectures on homosexuality that were receiving considerable, and sympathetic, coverage in the press.

Demise of the Early Homosexual Rights Movement

After 1923, the year of the final publication of the Scientific Humanitarian Committee's Yearbook, the fate of the early gay movement becomes sketchy and more difficult to trace.

Throughout the next decade, its members continued to speak out on gay rights and took an active part in the organization of congresses of the World League for Sexual Reform in 1928, 1929, and 1930. At its peak, over 130,000 persons belonged to organizations affiliated with the League.

A paper that dealt specifically with gay oppression at the 1928 congress in Copenhagen was a stirring "Appeal on Behalf of an Oppressed Variety of Human Being." It was written by Kurt Hiller, and read by Hirschfeld.

The World League for Sexual Reform took the position that homosexual acts should be treated the same legally as heterosexual acts, and it endorsed the stated principle of legal philosophy that there should be "no crimes without victims." Hirschfeld elaborated on the League's position on sexual legislation in a speech to the 1929 International Congress held in London:

"After the war, some European countries decided to issue a new sexual law. This has already been introduced and accepted in Russia,

Denmark and Turkey. Discussions about new laws for punishment of sexual offences have taken place in the penal law committees in Germany, Austria, Italy, Czecho-Slovakia and Switzerland. New plans for sexual legislation are being prepared in Poland, Yugo-Slavia, the Baltic states, as well as in several other post-war states.

"The *Russian* penal code has removed adultery, bigamy, homosexual intercourse, incest, sodomy, interruption of pregnancy, prostitution and concubinage from its list of punishable offences. The new German penal law bill, which has not yet been passed, shows greater punishments for 39 offences and lesser punishments for 13, compared to the sexual legislation valid today. Among the latter, offensive behavior is included.

"In sexual legislation, two principal views and systems are opposing one another: *The right of sexual guardianship and the right of sexual self-government*. The former represents the view that all sexual acts which do not serve propagation, legalised by marriage, are sinful and are to be rejected. This view reached its zenith between the 13th and 18th century and was enforced with extremely severe penalties of almost sadistic cruelty. Cambacérès, the creator of the Code Napoleon, completely abolished these regulations, chiefly from legal considerations. Only in the middle of last century, *scientific* points of view were considered in the judgment of sexual actions.

"As the country where this more modern attitude originated, Austria is to be named first, where Krafft-Ebing has caused, by his classical work 'Psychopathia Sexualis', a great change of opinion.

"Today, our standpoint is this: A crime is a crime whether it has been committed from sexual or other egotistical motives. Not sexuality itself, but the sexual action that wrongs the rights of a second person, is breaking the law and is therefore punishable. The sexual motive, according to its character, cannot be considered as an aggravating circumstance for punishment. In all penal codes, murder for lust is mentioned as murder and not as a sexual crime. Moreover, the other sexual crimes would have to be divided among the crimes which are committed against the rights of another person or if one thinks that one cannot do without threats of punishment, one paragraph should be added to the penal code, which might be worded as follows:

"Every one is to be punished: Who commits sexual actions against another person by force or by help [of] threats, against feeble-minded individuals, against individuals not yet matured, or in a way causing public offence.

"Punishment of all sexual actions which are not mentioned in the above would only give opportunities to blackmailers. The sexual minorities have their rights in much the same way as national minorities."

Hirschfeld continued his international speaking tours throughout the twenties, including a world trip beginning in 1930 that brought him to the United States and the Orient, including China. Upon his return to Europe, in 1932, he was forced by the threat of Hitlerism to remain outside Germany. He took refuge first in Switzerland, and then in France.

On May 6, 1933, a Berlin newspaper announced that the city's libraries were to be cleansed of books of "un-German" spirit, and that the students of the Gymnastic Academy would start with the Institute for Sexual Science. The Nazi newspaper hailed their destructive raid as a "deed of culture" aimed at an institution that "tried to shelter behind a scientific cloak and was always protected during the fourteen years of Marxist rule by the authorities of that period, [and] was an unparalleled breeding ground of dirt and filth. . . ."

The following eyewitness account of the fascist raid is taken from *The Brown Book of The Hitler Terror*:

"At 9:30 a.m. some lorries drew up in front of the Institute with about one hundred students and a brass band. They drew up in military formation in front of the Institute, and then marched into the building with their band playing. As the office was not yet open, there was no responsible person there; there were only a few women and one man. The students demanded admittance to every room, and broke in the doors of those which were closed, including the office of the World League for Sexual Reform. When they found that there was not much to be had in the lower rooms, they made their way up to the first floor, where they emptied the ink bottles over manuscripts and carpets and then made for the book-cases. They took away whatever they thought not completely unobjectionable, working for the most part on the basis of the so-called 'black list.' But they went beyond this, and took other books also, including for example a large work on Tutankhamen and a number of art journals which they found among the secretary's private books. They then removed from the archives the large charts dealing with intersexual cases, which had been prepared for the International Medical Congress held at the Kensington Museum in London in 1913. They threw most of these charts through the windows to their comrades who were standing outside. . . .

"The staff was kept under observation during the whole of the proceedings, and the band played throughout, so that a large crowd of inquisitive people gathered outside. At 12 o'clock the leader made a long speech, and then the gang left, singing a particularly vulgar song and also the Horst-Wessel song.

"At three o'clock a number of truckloads of storm troopers showed up and announced that they were going to continue the work begun that morning. This second troop then proceeded to make a careful search through every room, taking down to the lorries basket after basket of valuable books and manuscripts—two lorry-loads in all. It was clear from the oaths used that the names of the authors whose books were in the special library were well known to the students. Sigmund Freud, whose photograph they took from the staircase and carried off, was called 'that Jewish sow Freud'; and Havelock Ellis was called 'that swine.' Other English authors wanted by them were Oscar Wilde, Edward Carpenter, and Norman Haire; and also the works of Judge Lindsay, the American juvenile judge, Margaret Sanger, and George Silvester Viereck; and of French writers, the works of André Gide, Marcel Proust, Pierre Loti, Zola, etc. The sight of the works of the Danish doctor Leunbach also made them break out into oaths. Many bound volumes of periodicals were also removed. They also wanted to take away several thousand questionnaires which were among the records, but desisted when they were assured that these were simply medical histories. On the other hand, it did not prove possible to dissuade them from removing the material belonging to the World League of Sexual Reform, the whole edition of the journal *Sexus* and the card index. In addition, a great many manuscripts, including many unpublished ones, fell into their hands. . . ."

A few days later, all the books and photographs, together with a large number of other works, were publicly burned on Opera Square. More than 10,000 volumes from the Institute's special library were destroyed. A bust of Hirschfeld was carried in a torchlight procession and thrown onto the fire.

Nazis carry bust of Magnus Hirschfeld in torchlight procession.

In its obituary on Hirschfeld, the *New York Herald Tribune* referred to this incident. It noted that Hirschfeld, "famous as he was among scientists throughout the world, was persona non grata to the Nazis, and in May, 1933, in the week when the great bonfire in the square of the University of Berlin consumed thousands of Germany's literary and scientific treasures, a gang of students, obeying trumpet calls, stormed the Institute and confiscated half a ton of Dr. Hirschfeld's priceless books and pamphlets, the work of years, and fed them to the flames. Dr. Hirschfeld was then 'under protective custody.' The Institute was closed and Dr. Hirschfeld had been living in France for some time."

Magnus Hirschfeld eventually leased an apartment in Nice, where he began to rebuild what he hoped would become a replica of the Berlin Institute. He had hardly begun this project when he died.

From 1933 to 1935 the gay movement was brutally exterminated by both the fascists and the Stalinists.

The last of an irregular series of "Newsletters" of the Scientific Humanitarian Committee was published in February, 1933, by Kurt Hiller. In July of the same year, Hiller was arrested and sent to the Oranienburg concentration camp. He was fortunate to be released nine months later, after nearly dying from mistreatment in the concentration camp, and he left Germany.

The bourgeois media, as well as the Stalinist, have attempted to link fascism with the proliferation or tolerance of homosexuality. Nothing could be further from the truth. The real fascist position in sexual matters was expressed by their slogan, "moral purity"; and the fascist ideal was the familiar sexual repression ordained by Christian virtue. If on a political-economic level fascism was totalitarian monopoly capitalism, on the level of sexual morality, fascism was totalitarian Christianity. The sexual morality of the good fascist is laid down in the following selection from a fascist sex pamphlet, quoted in Wilhelm Reich's *The Mass Psychology of Fascism*:

"Homosexuality is the mark of Cain, of a godless and soulless culture which is sick to the core. It is the consequence of the prevailing view of the world and of life, the highest aim of which is love of pleasure. Professor Foerster has rightfully stated in his *Sexualethik*: 'Where spiritual heroism is made fun of and the sowing of one's wild oats is glorified, everything which is perverse, demonic and vile plucks up courage to manifest itself openly; indeed, it scoffs at the healthy as an illness and sets itself up as the standard of life.' "

Open Nazi terror against homosexuals began with the murders of Ernst Röhm (widely known to be homosexual) and other leaders of the SA (the Brown Shirts) from June 29 to July 1, 1934. The plebian

43

SA, recruited largely from the lumpenproletariat (i.e., sub-working class—the unemployables, bums, derelicts, criminal elements, etc.), had begun to pose a threat to Hitler's power, and the aristocratic Reichswehr officers corps and the capitalist ruling class had demanded it be dealt with.

In 1935, the Nazis extended Paragraph 175 to include kisses, embraces, and even homosexual fantasies. The utterly irrational nature of Nazi philosophy is perfectly illustrated by their being as concerned with what was allegedly in someone's head—with his "intent"—as with practice in the real world. This mystical nonsense was justified by a Nazi theory of "phenomenological justice" that purported to evaluate a person's character rather than his actions. Jim Steakley wrote in his article, "Homosexuals and the Third Reich" (*Body Politic*, No. 11, 1974):

"The 'healthy sensibility of the people' (*gesundes Volksempfinden*) was elevated to the highest normative legal concept, and the Nazis were thus in a position to prosecute an individual solely on the grounds of his sexual orientation. (After World War II, incidentally, this law was immediately stricken from the books in East Germany as a product of fascist thinking, while it remained on the books in West Germany.)"

Homosexuals by the tens of thousands were sent to concentration camps, where they were subjected to special abuse. Most of them perished. Beginning in 1934, homosexuals from other countries occupied by the Nazis were sent to concentration camps in Germany and Austria. Every prisoner in the camps was identified by an emblem indicating the reason he or she was interned—as a Jew, gypsy, socialist, communist, or homosexual. The insignia for homosexuals was a pink triangle, about two and three-quarters of an inch in height, worn on the left side of the jacket and on the right leg of the trousers.

Histories of Nazi rule have been unusually squeamish in dealing with the persecution of gay people, often not even mentioning it. Certainly tens of thousands, and more likely hundreds of thousands of homosexuals were murdered by the fascists. An exact estimate is impossible, because homosexuals, especially those in the military, were routinely shot without trial. The concentration camp records, which would have provided information, were systematically

44

destroyed when German defeat became apparent.

Not only has bourgeois history suppressed the story of how homosexuals were persecuted under fascism, but the mass media—movies like "The Damned," men's adventure magazines, war comics, etc.—have turned the victim into the criminal, through their false association of fascism with sexual "perversion."

Following the death of Magnus Hirschfeld, the two remaining presidents of the World League for Sexual Reform, Norman Haire and Dr. Leunbach, found it necessary to dissolve the League in 1935. With the rise of fascism, most of the European sections had ceased to function. Political differences among the members of the World League made it impossible to continue. In a letter announcing their decision, the two presidents explained the differences: Haire insisted "that all revolutionary activity should be kept out of the program of the WLSR," while Leunbach was "of the opinion that it is impossible to reach the goals of the WLSR without at the same time fighting for a socialist revolution." This act put the final touch on the demise of the early gay movement.

SCIENTIFIC AND THEORETICAL ISSUES

Much of the history of the early homosexual rights movement involved debate over theoretical and scientific questions. The entire Nineteenth Century witnessed intense struggle between advancing science and the old myths. The early geologists, sociologists, Darwinian evolutionists, and other scientists were all castigated in their time by frenzied spokesmen for Christianity and the established order as "infidels," "practitioners of the dark arts," etc. But science advanced, and with it, a challenge to the "eternal moral truths" of theological morality.

The first militant writer on the subject of homosexuality was Ulrichs. His greatest contribution was to break through the taboo of silence. What had once been "the sin so horrible that it must not be mentioned among Christians" (*peccatum illude horribile, inter Christianos non nominandum*) became an appropriate subject for discussion and objective evaluation.

Many of Ulrichs' ideas are no longer tenable, in particular his notion that homosexuality was congenital, that homosexuals represented a separate variety of human being ("Uranians"), that the male homosexual had "a feminine soul enclosed in a man's body" (*anima muliebris in corpore virili inclusa*). Clearly Ulrichs' outlook was idealistic in the extreme. His schema simply did not accord with reality.*

---

* In real life, for example, individuals could go from heterosexual to homosexual behavior, and *vice versa*; and further, male homosexuals were by no means always feminine in appearance or otherwise. To resolve these contradictions, Ulrichs was forced to devise a most elaborate, indeed metaphysical, system of classification.

Human males were divided into three main categories: (a) the Normal Man or Dioning—called Uraniaster when he acquires Urning tendencies (!); (b) Urnings; and (c) Urano-dionings—those *born* with a capacity for love in both directions.

Urnings were further divided into four sub-categories: (1) the *Männling*, who

Erroneous though Ulrichs' concepts were, they made it possible to reject the old notions of sin, depravity, or morbidity. Homosexuality was just as natural and healthy for an Urning as heterosexuality was for a Dioning. On this basis it was possible to agitate against the barbarity of laws which persecuted a variety of human being merely for being different. And since everything was congenital, no threat to the normalcy of Dionings was involved. Although these ideas of Ulrichs' are now thoroughly refuted by the unified evidence of history, anthropology, zoology, depth psychology, and statistical research, it is important to be aware of them, since they left their mark upon several decades of ideology—especially in medical literature—and upon popular thinking.

Richard von Krafft-Ebing incorporated many of Ulrichs' ideas into his *Psychopathia Sexualis*, the first sexological best-seller. Krafft-Ebing considered homosexuality, with all other sexual deviations, to be the product of hereditary degeneration of the central nervous system. His system of classification for homosexuals was fully as elaborate and idealistic as Ulrichs'. On the positive side, Krafft-Ebing later considerably modified his view that homosexuality was always a disease; he supported the petition to repeal Paragraph 175. His case histories provided valuable data for later psychologists, notably Sigmund Freud.

Magnus Hirschfeld developed the concept of sexual *Zwischenstufen* or intermediate states, sharing with Ulrichs the notion that homosexuality represented an inborn human variation. He went even

is thoroughly manly in appearance, mental habit, and character; (2) is the *Zwischen-Urning*, who is an intermediate type; (3) the *Weibling*, who is effeminate in appearance and cast of mind; and (4) the "Virilized Urning," an Urning who acquires the normal habit (!!).

Rigid and artificial though Ulrichs' system of classification was, however, he nevertheless showed some awareness that the potential for homosexual love exists in everyone (though even here, he tended to approach the question from a physiological and biological, rather than historical and sociological, angle). In a letter of December 23, 1862, for instance, he wrote:

"Sexual dualism, which is universally present in embryonic form in every human individual, simply reaches a higher degree of expression in hermaphrodites and uranians than in the ordinary man and woman. With uranians, this level of expression merely takes a different form than with hermaphrodites."

47

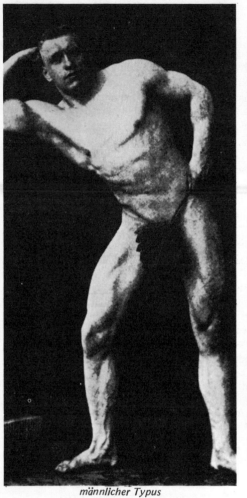

männlicher Typus

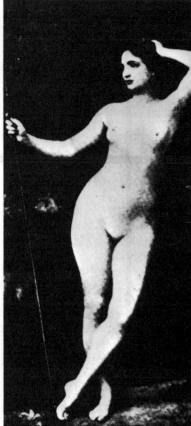

weiblicher Typus

(Published as a fold-out in Vol. I of the 1903 issue of the Yearbook, these three photographs depict the static and now discredited view of the Scientific Humanitarian Committee that the sexual orientation of human beings corresponded to physical types: 1— the male type (i.e., heterosexual male); 2— female type (i.e., heterosexual female); 3— uranian type (i.e., homosexual person, seen as a "third sex" that combined physiological elements of the "male" and "female" types).

urnischer Typus

further than Ulrichs to consider the bodies of homosexuals also to be sexually intermediate. Reflecting Hirschfeld's viewpoints, the Yearbook of the Scientific Humanitarian Committee was entitled the *Yearbook for Intermediate Sexual Types, with particular attention to homosexuality.*

Hirschfeld's viewpoints were not shared by everyone in the gay movement. In 1907, when the group led by Benedict Friedländer split from the Scientific Humanitarian Committee, it was largely because of differences over scientific questions. Friedländer felt that Hirschfeld's theories held back the movement and declared: "The way is free for a less dogmatic, more open and more correct evaluation of homosexual love."

The *Zwischenstufen* theory was attacked by Friedländer as "degrading and a beggarly . . . pleading for sympathy." He ridiculed the notion of "a poor womanly soul languishing away in a man's body, and of the 'third sex.' " Friedländer insisted upon a historical approach which also took into account anthropological evidence; he wrote, "A glance at the cultures of countries before and outside of Christianity suffices to show the complete untenability of the [*Zwischenstufen*] theory. Especially in ancient Greece, most of the military leaders, artists, and thinkers would have had to be 'psychic hermaphrodites.' "

The medical profession came in for scathing analysis by Friedländer, who considered the prominence of its representatives in the gay movement to be harmful. He wrote, "Now with diseases, one can certainly have pity, one can behave humanely to the sick and indeed try to 'heal' them; at no time does one acknowledge presumed physical inferiors as having equal rights."

Friedländer strongly rejected the distinctions certain idealist authorities made between "true" and "pseudo" homosexuality, saying " . . . it is incomprehensible what is 'pseudo' about it." Also, he clearly anticipated Kinsey's concept of the sexual continuum. He considered bisexuality to be the fullest and least distorted human condition. Friedländer's death in 1908 cut short his contributions. Hirschfeld, describing the Friedländer secession in the 1908 Yearbook, was none too generous. Fearful of seeing gays accused of attempting to "convert" to homosexuality, he unjustly branded

50

Friedländer's bisexuality theory as "water in the mill of the enemy."

After 1910, however, Hirschfeld became much less sectarian and much more open to a historical perspective, and he became increasingly anticlerical, attacking as an enemy the "theological sexual outlook," though he never totally abandoned his belief that homosexuality was largely congenital. His surveys in 1903 were pioneering efforts, however antiquated they might seem in the light of present-day statistical laws and survey techniques. Hirschfeld's leadership in the foundation of the Institute for Sexual Science and the World League for Sexual Reform far outweigh the errors of his earlier theories.

In England, two writers deserve mention. One, Sir Richard Burton, was the translator of the *Arabian Nights*. His "Terminal Essay" on pederasty, published in volume 10 of the *Arabian Nights* in 1885, constituted a powerful defense of homosexual love, using a vast amount of historical and anthropological evidence, as well as his own observations in Africa and the East.

Havelock Ellis' great work, *Studies In the Psychology of Sex*, was most influential, and provided an immense amount of all kinds of information—historical, anthropological, case studies, and other data. When the volume on *Sexual Inversion* was published in 1898, he was immediately prosecuted, and his printer was heavily fined.*

---

* Since this time, sufficient evidence has accumulated—from anthropology, history, zoology, psychology, statistical research, sociology, the Kinsey studies, and studies of one-sex groups—that without hesitation, one can now describe homosexuality as a basic component of the human animal. There is nothing whatever wrong with homosexuality; in no way is it opposed to or incompatible with heterosexuality. Homosexual behavior occurs because it is part of healthy human sexual potential, not because of physical or psychic hermaphroditism, hormonal imbalance, unhappy childhoods, depravity, societal decadence, or any of the other explanations devised by priests, psychiatrists and others of their ilk.

What needs to be explained is not homosexuality, but rather the taboo against it, and the persecution of homosexuals. Basically, the antihomosexual taboo is a part of the Judeo-Christian code of sexual morality, and, with the exception of Zoroastrianism (a religion of ancient Persia), antihomosexual prejudice and repression have been limited to cultures under the influence of Judeo-Christianity.

SOCIALISM AND THE EARLY GAY MOVEMENT

An Early Encounter

One encounter between socialism and the gay issue goes back to the early 1860s, a generation before the first organized gay movement, a period when the death penalty for male homosexual acts was just being removed in England and still in effect in Scotland. The lawyer, J. B. von Schweitzer, got in trouble over homosexual activity in Mannheim. He was brought to trial, punished, and disbarred from the legal profession. He was helped out of his impasse by Ferdinand Lassalle, who encouraged him to re-enter politics. Schweitzer joined Lassalle's Universal German Workingmen's Association in 1863.

Several members of the Association were offended by the Schweitzer incident. Ferdinand Lassalle, however, defended Schweitzer, and said, "What Schweitzer did isn't pretty, but I hardly look upon it as a crime. At any rate, we can't let ourselves lose someone with such great ability, indeed a phenomenal person. In the long run, sexual activity is a matter of taste and ought to be left up to each person, so long as he doesn't encroach upon someone else's interests. Though I wouldn't give my daughter in marriage to such a man."

After Lassalle's death, Schweitzer was elected head of the Universal German Workingmen's Association. The German workers apparently were more impressed by Schweitzer's abilities as a working-class leader than by any past indiscretion in his personal life. He was later elected as a representative in the Reichstag.

The Oscar Wilde Trial and *Die Neue Zeit*

Oscar Wilde was at the height of his success when he was arrested in April 1895. He was charged with homosexual offenses under the

Criminal Law Amendment Act of 1885, which dealt with "gross indecencies" committed either in public or private. This followed the collapse of Wilde's prosecution of the Marquess of Queensberry (the father of his young lover) for criminal libel, in which Queensberry had successfully pleaded justification for calling Wilde a "sodomite" by bringing forward evidence, mostly from male prostitutes, that Wilde was indeed a "sodomite."

The case was one of the most sensational in English history. The British press was unanimous in its condemnation of Wilde, rousing public opinion to a frenzy of vilification against him. He was called "the most depraved man in the world," and worse things. Pamphlets attacking him were hawked in the streets of London.

An atmosphere of deepest reaction ensued for homosexuals. To the hysterical populace, sodomy was portrayed as an evil so fearful, so loathsome, that surely there could not exist more than a few men in London capable of it; yet at the same time, sodomy was felt to be so powerfully contagious that if the vice were not repressed with the utmost severity, the entire youth of the city would become infected.

Wilde's defense in his trial was necessarily an attempt to prove he had not committed the homosexual acts he was charged with, and that he had no inclination to commit such acts. The time was hardly ripe to claim the *right to practice homosexual love*. Nevertheless, Wilde was moved during cross-examination to defend "the love that dare not speak its name," a phrase from a poem the prosecution attempted to link to Wilde. Following is the exchange from the trial:

Prosecutor: Is it not clear that the love described related to natural and unnatural love?

Wilde: No.

Prosecutor: What is the love that dare not speak its name?

Wilde: "The Love that dare not speak its name" in this century is such a great affection of an elder for a younger man as there was between David and Jonathan, such as Plato made the very basis of his philosophy, and such as you find in the sonnets of Michelangelo and Shakespeare. It is that deep, spiritual affection that is as pure as it is perfect. It dictates and pervades great works of art like those of Shakespeare and Michelangelo, and those two letters of mine, such as

Oscar Wilde in 1889.

they are. It is in this century misunderstood, so much misunderstood that it may be described as the "Love that dare not speak its name," and on account of it I am placed where I am now. It is beautiful, it is fine, it is the noblest form of affection. There is nothing unnatural about it. It is intellectual, and it repeatedly exists between an elder and a younger man, when the elder man has intellect, and the younger man has all the joy, hope and glamour of life before him. That it should be so, the world does not understand. The world mocks at it and sometimes puts one in the pillory for it.

This speech caused a loud burst of applause to erupt from the gallery of the courtroom. The judge, Mr. Justice Charles, was forced to declare, "If there is the slightest manifestation of feeling I shall have the Court cleared. There must be complete silence observed." The jury was unable to agree on a verdict. Wilde's speech was said to have left an unforgettable impression on all who heard it, and it may have moved at least one juror to hold out against a conviction.

On his retrial, Wilde was faced with a far more vindictive prosecutor, the Solicitor-General himself, Sir Frank Lockwood, and with a bigoted and unfair judge, Mr. Justice Wills. The judge's "charge to the jury" was hardly impartial, his opening statements being: "Gentlemen of the jury, this case is a most difficult one, and my task very severe. I would rather try the most shocking murder case that it has ever fallen to my lot to try than be engaged in a case of this description," and he referred to the "horrible nature of the charges involved."

Wilde was found guilty. Mr. Justice Wills went immediately to sentencing, over the objection of Wilde's lawyer. He did so in a speech reflecting the tenor of the times:

Mr. Justice Wills: Oscar Wilde and Alfred Taylor [Wilde's co-defendant], the crime of which you have been convicted is so bad that one has to put stern restraint upon one's self to prevent one's self from describing, in language which I would rather not use, the sentiments which must rise to the breast of every man of honour who has heard the details of these two terrible trials. That the jury have arrived at a correct verdict in this case I cannot persuade myself to entertain the shadow of a doubt; and I hope, at all events, that those who sometimes imagine that a judge is half-hearted in the cause of decency and morality because he takes care no prejudice shall enter into the case, may see that that is consistent at least with the utmost sense of indignation at the horrible charges brought home to both of you.

It is no use for me to address you. People who can do these things must be dead to all sense of shame, and one cannot hope to produce any effect upon them. It is the worst case I have ever tried. That you, Taylor, kept a kind of male brothel it is impossible to doubt. And that you, Wilde, have been the centre of a circle of extensive corruption of the most hideous kind among young men, it is equally impossible to doubt.

I shall, under such circumstances, be expected to pass the severest sentence that the law allows. In my judgement it is totally inadequate for such a case as this. The sentence is that each of you be imprisoned and kept to hard labour for two years.

[Some cries of "Oh! Oh!" and "Shame" were heard in Court.]

Oscar Wilde: And I? May I say nothing, my lord?

[His lordship made no reply beyond a wave of the hand to the warders, who hurried the prisoners out of sight.]

In 1896, George Bernard Shaw attempted to get a petition going calling for the mitigation or termination of the sentence Wilde was then serving. The effort failed; Shaw was unable to get any people of note to co-sponsor the petition other than a fellow Fabian socialist and a History professor at Oxford, and he was afraid that without more representative sponsorship, the petition would get nowhere.

A number of French citizens initiated a petition to the Queen of England to pardon Wilde, but Queen Victoria issued no pardon. The French press, by and large, while not abusing Wilde, treated the whole thing in an ironical and sarcastic tone. Only a few writers raised their voices in defense of Wilde.

Wilde was bankrupt and ruined. He died three years after release from prison. The Scientific Humanitarian Committee's Yearbook of 1901 contained a biography by Numa Praetorius (Eugen Wilhelm); Magnus Hirschfeld described Wilde as "a martyr to his individuality."

The Wilde case vividly brought home the reality of oppression to homosexuals, and it may have kindled gay anger and provided a spark for an activist homosexual rights movement. In addition to the considerable international repercussions of the case, direct contact occurred in 1896, when Wilde was in prison, between his most trusted friend, Robert Ross, and Hirschfeld, who was soon to go on to found the Scientific Humanitarian Committee.

In the popular mind, Oscar Wilde is still seen as a stereotyped fop, dilletante, and poseur. But Wilde was a social critic with a radical sensibility. He wrote a long essay, *The Soul of Man Under Socialism*, in which he envisioned the opportunities socialism would present for the advancement of human culture. It was not orthodox Marxist socialism by any means, but the ruling classes did not find it any more endearing on this account. According to Wilde's friend and biographer, Robert Sherard, millions of copies of the pamphlet were sold in Central and Eastern Europe; it gained a reputation among the oppressed and exploited classes under the despotisms in Russia, Germany, and Austria; and large pirated editions were sold by revolutionary groups in America.

He was the only literary figure in London willing to sign a petition on behalf of the Haymarket martyrs. Bernard Shaw describes this in a letter to Frank Harris, a mutual friend of his and Wilde's:

"What first established a friendly feeling in me was, unexpectedly enough, the affair of the Chicago anarchists. ... I tried to get some literary men in London, all heroic rebels and skeptics on paper, to sign a memorial asking for the reprieve of these unfortunate men. The only signature I got was Oscar's. It was a completely disinterested act on his part; and it secured my distinguished consideration for him for the rest of his life."

Many of Wilde's works, even his fashionable plays, contained passages of radical social criticism. His work following release from prison, the poem *The Ballad of Reading Gaol*, and several letters to newspapers, were protests against the injustices of the British prison system. In the climactic stanzas of *The Ballad of Reading Gaol*, Wilde's protest against the prison system is extended to an indictment of the entire social system:

I know not whether Laws be right,
  Or whether Laws be wrong;
All that we know who lie in gaol
  Is that the wall is strong;
And that each day is like a year,
  A year whose days are long.

But this I know, that every Law
  That men have made for Man,
Since first Man took his brother's life,
  And the sad world began,
But straws the wheat and saves the chaff
  With a most evil fan.

This too I know—and wise it were
  If each could know the same—
That every prison that men build
  Is built with bricks of shame,
And bound with bars lest Christ should see
  How men their brothers maim.

In Germany, in *Die Neue Zeit*, the most prestigious journal of the Second International, Eduard Bernstein defended Oscar Wilde. In the long, two-part article written in April-May 1895, Bernstein presented a far-ranging materialist critique of the irrationality and hypocrisy of society's sexual morality, the legal contradictions and injustices, the obligation of the socialist movement to provide leadership on sexual questions from a scientific perspective.

He wrote, "Although the subject of sex life might seem of low priority for the economic and political struggle of the Social Democracy, this nevertheless does not mean it is not obligatory to find a standard also for judging this side of social life, a standard based on a scientific approach and knowledge rather than on more or less arbitrary moral concepts. Today the party is strong enough to exert an influence on the character of statutory law, and through its speakers and its press it enjoys an influence upon public opinion that extends beyond the circle of its own supporters. As a result, it must take a certain responsibility for what happens these days. Therefore, an attempt will be made in what follows to open up the way to such a scientific approach to the problem."

Bernstein argued that the word "unnatural," as applied legally and in common parlance to homosexual acts, was inappropriate. Strictly speaking, nothing one did in the course of a day was "natural," including carrying on "intercourse" through the written word. He proposed instead saying "not the norm," emphasizing the materialist basic that *"moral attitudes are historical phenomena."* Judgments on what acts are "natural" or "unnatural" really reflect a society's stage of development rather than any genuine state of nature.

Bernstein took up and refuted the popular notion that an increase in homosexuality accompanied so-called periods of decadence, arguing that the ancient Greeks and other peoples had freely allowed and practiced homosexual love in the periods of their greatest vitality.

Bernstein warned against accepting sickness theories put forward by Krafft-Ebing and the majority of the psychiatrists of that day. He stressed that psychiatrists have difficulty judging an individual case of same-sex love on truly medical rather than on moralizing grounds. He wrote: "In any case, it is a certainty that [male homosexuality] is by no means always a sign of a depraved disposition, decrepitude, bestial pleasure-seeking and the like. Anyone who comes out with such [psychiatric] epithets takes the standpoint of the most reactionary penal laws."

Throughout Bernstein's article runs the insistence that sexual mores be seen in historical perspective, illuminated by anthropology and ethnology, rather than in absolute, idealist terms. He observed, " ... previously the Romans, the Greeks, the Egyptians and various Asiatic peoples cultivated homosexual gratification." Reserving judgment on how this first came about, he continued: " ... we must be satisfied with the statement that same-sex intercourse is so old and so widespread that there is no stage of human culture we could say with certainty were free from this phenomenon."

Bernstein's defense of Oscar Wilde and his exposition of the historical-materialist position on homosexuality in *Die Neue Zeit* was nothing short of remarkable at the time; it must stand as one of the best and most advanced expositions on the subject of homosexuality to come out of the socialist movement.

The Social Democrats and the 1905 Reichstag Debate

August Bebel continued to support the gay movement following his 1898 stand. In a 1907 speech, the old and ailing Bebel recalled the shock some Reichstag members had expressed over his estimates as to the great numbers of homosexuals, and how he had been accused of exaggeration. In retrospect, Bebel maintained he had not exaggerated —if anything he may have estimated too few!

Bebel also stressed that Paragraph 175 was enforced with a double standard—one for the higher-ups and another for workers. In his opinion, on this basis alone, Paragraph 175 was indefensible.

He wound up by saying, "But gentlemen, you have no idea how many respectable, honorable and brave men, even in high and the highest positions, are driven to suicide year after year, one from shame, another from fear of the blackmailer."

It reflects Bebel's greatness that he could respond to, learn from, and evolve with the rise of the gay movement. Following his lead, the Social Democracy supported the petition to repeal Paragraph 175, and the Party's newspaper *Vorwärts*, carried news of the gay movement.

An unprecedented parliamentary debate on gay rights took place on May 31, 1905, with the Social Democrats intervening in a most vigorous way. The Reichstag split nearly down the middle—the Social Democrats supporting the petition and nearly all members of the clerical and bourgeois parties opposing it.

The brunt of the argument for the gay movement's petition to repeal Paragraph 175 was carried by the Social Democrat Adolph Thiele, who had obviously done considerable research and collaborated with the Scientific Humanitarian Committee. His speeches take up a full thirty-four pages of the Committee's 1905 Yearbook, which printed the entire record of the debate.

Thiele expressed his hope that the matter could be approached in as objective, unprejudiced, and non-partisan a way as possible. He described the petition, which then had about 5,000 signers.

Using Magnus Hirschfeld's statistical investigations, which indicated that about 6 percent of the population were either homo- or bisexual (a much too low figure in light of the Kinsey studies), he argued that not just thousands, but *hundreds of thousands* of Germans were made miserable and exposed to blackmail because of Paragraph 175.

Thiele attributed such laws as Paragraph 175 to carry-overs from the "priestly cruelty and intolerance" of the Middle Ages. He said the treatment of gays "reminds one of the period of the Middle Ages, of that time when witches were burned, heretics were tortured, and proceedings against dissenters were conducted with the wheel and gallows."

The opposition to the petition was led by a Dr. Thaler of the Center Party, which reflected the views of the Roman Catholic Church and which was the leading political opponent of homosexual rights. Thaler's arguments included a vicious personal attack on Karl Ulrichs; the brilliant observation that although 5,000 Germans had signed the petition 60 million had *not* signed it!; and an endorsement of the viewpoints of Moses, St. Paul, and Justinian. Dr. Thaler concluded his presentation by pleading, "So let's keep respect for Paragraph 175 to protect the threatened morals and the vitality of the German people."

The Left Queer-baits the Nazis

Despite their earlier record of support for gay rights, the Social Democrats—and the left as a whole—fell into the unpardonable error, during the rise of the Nazis, of attempting to use homosexuality against the fascists. Few voices were heard in the early thirties in defense of homosexuals against the vicious slanders and persecution that accompanied the growing fascist menace. One voice, however, was that of the writer, Kurt Tucholsky, who attacked the left for its myopic and self-defeating approach to the issue of homosexuality:

"For some time, the radical left-wing press has been running accusations, jokes, and cutting remarks about Captain Röhm, a functionary of the Hitler movement [and head of the SA]. Röhm is, as is known, homosexual. The carryings on against him take as their starting point material published by the 'Münchner Post,' which revealed this fact about him. The 'Münchner Post' also published a letter in which Röhm wrote about his tendency to a friend. Röhm's letter might just as well have appeared in Psychopathia sexualis; it was not even distasteful. I consider these attacks against this man to be rather indecent. Apparently, any means, fair or foul, can be used against Hitler and his people. Yet anyone who so mercilessly deals with others in this fashion is entitled to no consideration whatever—Let him have it! In this connection too I haven't let the personal life of the parties concerned keep me from doing what had to be done—I have always gone after them with might and main! But this present business is going too far. And it is on behalf of people like us that it is going too far. Above all, one should not go searching out one's adversaries in their beds. The only thing that might be permissible is the following: To point to those remarks by the Nazis in which they deal with the 'eastern vices' of the post-war period as if homosexuality, lesbian love, and such things had been invented by the Russians and then infiltrated into the noble, unspoiled, pure German people. If a Nazi says this kind of thing, then—and only then—is it permissible to say: You have homosexuals in your own movement who admit their proclivities, who are indeed proud of them—so shut up!

"Yet the jokes about Röhm leave a bad taste in my mouth. His personal tastes can hardly be used as an argument against the man. He could be a completely decent man, so long as he does not misuse his position to get persons who are under his authority into bed with him—and there is not the slightest evidence that he does. We are fighting against the infamous Paragraph 175 in whatever way we can, but we have no right to join in with the chorus of those who would prefer to outlaw a man simply because he is homosexual.

"Has Röhm aroused public scandal? No. Has he gone after small boys? No. Has he been known to spread venereal disease? No.

"That, and that alone, might justify public criticism. All the rest is his own business."*

The Bolsheviks and the Stalinists

The Bolshevik government did away with all laws against

---

* Quoted from the German magazine *Him* (January 1973) in which this 1930s article was reprinted.

homosexual acts *per se* in December 1917. It viewed this act—along with other moves to extend sexual freedom—as an integral part of the social revolution. The sweeping reforms in sex-related matters that were an immediate by-product of the Russian Revolution ushered in a new atmosphere of sexual freedom. This atmosphere, which gave an impetus to the sexual reform movement in Western Europe and America, was consciously extended to include homosexuality. "It was necessary, it was said, to take down the walls which separated the homosexuals from the rest of society," Reich reported. This attitude was generally shared by the population. The official Soviet attitude under the Bolsheviks was that homosexuality did nobody any harm and that it was, if anything, a scientific matter, not a legal one.

The Bolshevik approach is reflected in a pamphlet by Dr. Grigorii Batkis, the Director of the Moscow Institute of Social Hygiene, entitled *The Sexual Revolution in Russia*. The German edition was published in 1925, the original Russian, in 1923. Batkis attended congresses of the World League for Sexual Reform in an official capacity. *The Sexual Revolution in Russia* covers a wide range of topics—basic theory, the tsarist legislation, women's emancipation, the family, protection of mothers and children, and the attitude of the state toward sexual activity. The following are some paragraphs from the introductory section of Batkis' pamphlet:

"The present sexual legislation in the Soviet Union is the work of the October Revolution. This revolution is important not only as a political phenomenon, which secures the political rule of the working class. But also for the revolutions which emanating from it reach out into all areas of life. . . .

"The social legislation of the Russian communist revolution does not intend to be a product of pure theoretical knowledge, but rather represents the outcome of experience. After the successful revolution, after the triumph of practice over theory, people first strove for new, firm regulations along economic lines. Along with this were created models governing family life and forms of sexual relations responding to the needs and natural demands of the people. . . .

"The war set in motion the broad masses, the 100 million peasants. New circumstances brought with them a new life and new outlook. In the first period of the war, women won economic independence both in the factory and in the country—but the October Revolution first cut the Gordian knot, and instead of mere reform, it completely revolutionized the laws. The revolution let nothing remain of the old despotic and infinitely unscientific laws; it did not tread the path of reformist bourgeois legislation which, with juristic subtlety, still hangs on to the concept of property in the sexual sphere, and ultimately demands that the double standard hold sway over sexual life. These laws always come about by disregarding science.

"The Soviet legislation proceeded along a new and previously untrodden path, in order to satisfy the new goals and tasks of the social revolution.

"No society in the whole world set these goals, whose problems confronted no previous revolution.

"The relationship of Soviet law to the sexual sphere is based on the principle that the demands of the vast majority of the people correspond to and are in harmony with the findings of contemporary science. . . .

"Now by taking into account all these aspects of the transition period, Soviet legislation bases itself on the following principle:

"It declares the absolute non-interference of the state and society into sexual matters, so long as nobody is injured, and no one's interests are encroached upon." (Emphasis in original.)

One paragraph of Batkis' pamphlet specifically deals with homosexuality:

"Concerning homosexuality, sodomy, and various other forms of sexual gratification, which are set down in European legislation as offenses against public morality—Soviet legislation treats these exactly the same as so-called 'natural' intercourse. All forms of sexual intercourse are private matters. Only when there's use of force or duress, as in general when there's an injury or encroachment upon the rights of another person, is there a question of criminal prosecution."

The work of Magnus Hirschfeld, and to a lesser extent Freud, provided much of the basis for the lengthy treatment of homosexuality in the first edition of the Great Soviet Encyclopedia, published in 1930.

The Encyclopedia noted that "in the advanced capitalist countries, the struggle for the abolition of these hypocritical laws is at present far from over. In Germany, for example, Magnus Hirschfeld is leading an especially fierce and not unsuccessful struggle to abolish the law against homosexuality. Soviet law does not recognize 'crime' against morality. . . ."*

Yet however commendable and tolerant their legal approach to homosexuality, and however advanced their social attitude in comparison to the capitalist world, there is no indication that the Soviets reached a point of attempting to positively integrate homosexual behavior into society: "It is already obvious that the Soviet evaluation of the features and characteristics of homosexuals is completely different from the West's evaluation. While understanding the wrongness of the development of homosexuality, society does not place and cannot place blame for it on those who exhibit it. This breaks down to a significant degree the wall which actually arises between the homosexual and society and forces the former to delve deeply into himself."

An event worth noting in connection with the new atmosphere was the publication, in 1920, of a collection of erotic verse by the Russian poet Mikhail Kuzmin. The collection, *Zanaveshannye Kartinki*, was illustrated with a few homoerotic drawings by a friend, Vladimir Milashevski. Although the booklet (which was privately printed) was published in the Soviet Union, Amsterdam is listed as the place of publication on the title page. Kuzmin, the first Russian writer of note to make homosexual love into a central theme of his work, continued to publish throughout the 1920s, his last work being published in 1929. His lover was executed during the Stalinist reaction in the thirties, and Kuzmin himself was reportedly on the list of those to be executed when he died in 1936. His reaction as a homosexual to the antihomosexuality of the Stalinists is unknown; his papers lie in Soviet archives open only to a select few.

---

* The line had changed considerably by the third edition of the Great Soviet Encyclopedia, published in 1971. The entry in its entirety: "*Homosexuality* (from *gomo* . . . and Lat. *sexus*—sex), a *sexual perversion* consisting in unnatural attraction to persons of the same sex. It occurs in persons of both sexes. The penal statutes of the USSR, the socialist countries and even some bourgeois states, provide for the punishment of homosexuality (*muzhelozhestvo*—sodomy between males)."

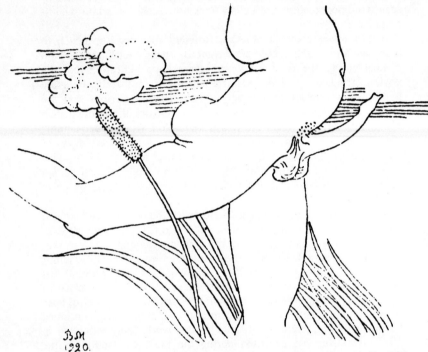

Illustration by Vladimir Milashevski for Zanaveshannye Kartinki *(1920) by Mikhail Kuzmin.*

The Soviet Union sent delegates to the International Congresses of the World League for Sexual Reform: Berlin (1921), Copenhagen (1928), London (1929), and Vienna (1930). A fifth congress—orginally scheduled to be held in Moscow, with point number one on the agenda being "Marxism and Sexual Problems"—was held in Brno, Czechoslovakia, in 1932 instead.

At the 1928 Congress in Copenhagen, the Soviet Union's sexual legislation was held up as a model in two resolutions passed by the congress, one dealing with the German penal code and the other offered as a model for world sexual reform.

At the same time, some indications of the advancing reaction became apparent in 1928. While still stressing the legality of homosexual acts *per se* and of abortions, the Professor Dr. Nikolai Pasche-Oserski also anticipated a legal reversal by referring to homosexuality as a potential "social peril" and abortions as an "evil." Pasche-Oserski suggested that the pragmatic "social peril" guideline might be more progressive than the traditional legal concept that no act should be considered a crime unless there is a law on the books stating so. Actually, "social peril" was a completely reactionary conception shared alike by the Stalinists and the bourgeoisie, throwing the door wide open to the exercise of arbitrary bureaucratic authority and the abrupt termination of civil liberties and legal safeguards.*

By the 1929 Congress in London, the Soviet delegates did not mention homosexuality, whereas before they had held up its non-criminal status in Soviet law as a model. In a related issue, Dr. A. Gens, while still maintaining that abortion as such was not punishable, referred to abortion as "an evil" to be agitated against among the masses of female toilers. Gens concluded his presentation, "Demand for Abortion in Soviet Russia," by stating: "We are deeply convinced that the best foundation of society necessitates the consciousness of motherhood."

At the 1930 Congress in Vienna, the Soviet delegates did not mention homosexuality either. Dr. Batkis now found himself put on the defensive, having to try to justify changes in attitude regarding abortion.

The German Communist Party, nevertheless, showed a willingness around this time (not destined to last long) to link its aims with the homosexual rights cause. In response to a query by Adolf Brand, addressed to the political parties represented on a Reichstag committee that was drawing up a penal reform measure in 1928, the

---

* "Social peril" was echoed in the French government's decision in 1960 to brand homosexuality as a "social scourge," and the Cuban decision in 1971 to treat it as a "social pathology."

Party noted its repeated support in the past for a repeal of the antihomosexual paragraph. The most active member of the Scientific Humanitarian Committee during the late twenties, Richard Linsert, was an anti-Stalinist member of the Party. And in 1930-31, the Party went so far as to agree to the organization of an association based on the sex-political program of Wilhelm Reich, then a Party member.

The group that resulted was called the Deutscher Reichsverband für Proletarische Sexualpolitik (German Association for Proletarian Sexual Politics), or Sexpol. It attained a membership of more than 20,000, and included as one of the main planks in its platform the demand for the abolition of the law against homosexuality. (This occurred during what is known as the ultraleft "third period" of the Communist International, a tactical zigzag in Stalinist policy.)

By 1931 and 1932, the increasing membership of Reich's Sexpol, and the growing support for struggle around issues relating to sex and mental hygiene, aroused increasing hostility within the Party leadership. Even before the Party was defeated by Hitler, it repudiated Reich and ordered all his works removed from its bookstores and banned their sale within its organizations. According to Reich, this policy originated in the leadership of the Party and was opposed by some of the rank and file.

Meanwhile, in the USSR, the Stalinists had begun to develop a whole mythology in which homosexuality was "the product of decadence in the bourgeois sector of society" and "the fascist perversion." (The fascists reciprocated by branding any departure from their glorified "moral purity" as "sexual Bolshevism"!) The Stalinists began to extol the virtues of "proletarian decency." Discrimination, spying, denunciation, and Party purges against homosexuals began. In some cases, old Bolsheviks like Klara Zetkin intervened and achieved acquittal.

In January 1934, mass arrests of gays were carried out in Moscow, Leningrad, Kharkov, and Odessa. Among those arrested were a great many actors, musicians, and other artists. They were accused of engaging in "homosexual orgies," and were sentenced to several years of imprisonment or exile to Siberia. The mass arrests produced a panic among Soviet gays, and were followed by numerous suicides in the Red Army itself.

In March 1934, a law punishing homosexual acts with imprisonment up to eight years was introduced. The law, which took the form of a federal statute, was the result of the personal intervention of Stalin. It limited the definition of homosexuality to males; it provided for up to five years imprisonment for consensual homosexual acts and up to eight years if the act was accompanied by taking advantage of the dependent position of one of the partners, by the use of force, or if it was conducted as a profession or publicly. All republics were required to insert the statute unchanged into their codes. In effect, the law raised homosexuality to the level of a state security matter, constituting a peril to the moral fabric of society.

The Soviet press began a campaign against homosexuality as a sign of "degeneracy of the fascist bourgeoisie." One of the loudest voices raised against homosexuality was that of the hack, Maxim Gorki, who also at this time lent his enthusiastic backing to the stifling, tasteless, and reactionary concept of "socialist realism." His article, "Proletarian humanism," speaks for itself: "One revolts at even mentioning the horrors [anti-Semitism and homosexuality] which fascism brings to such a rich flowering." And, he continued: "In the fascist countries, homosexuality, which ruins youth, flourishes without punishment; in the country where the proletariat has audaciously achieved social power, homosexuality has been declared a social crime and is heavily punished. There is already a slogan in Germany, 'Eradicate the homosexual and fascism will disappear.' " In truth, it was in June 1934, only three months after Stalin's antihomosexual statute was decreed, that Hitler wiped out the entire leadership of the SA, using arguments similar to those of the Soviet Union's antigay persecution.

The repressive campaign against homosexuality did not occur in isolation, of course, but went together with a general reactionary trend that accompanied the triumph of Stalinism. This was reflected in other areas, too, such as the abolition of legal abortion in 1936, and the exaltation of heterosexuality and the family as ideals for the Soviet citizen. A *Pravda* editorial discussing the proposal to abolish abortion painted a picture of the Stalinist citizen that, however revolting it might seem even to the heterosexually oriented person, certainly must have struck anguish and terror in the hearts of

Communist gays: "The *elite* of our country, the best of the Soviet youth, are as a rule also excellent family men who dearly love their children. And *vice versa*: the man who does not take marriage seriously, and abandons his children to the whims of fate, is usually also a bad worker and a poor member of society.

"Fatherhood and motherhood have long been virtues in this country. This can be seen at the first glance, without searching enquiry. Go through the parks and streets of Moscow or of any other town in the Soviet Union on a holiday, and you will see not a few young men walking with pink-cheeked well-fed babies in their arms."

It was during this period—at the end of 1935 and the first part of 1936—that the French writer, André Gide, made a visit to the USSR that wounded both his communist and his homosexual sensibilities. Homosexuals, he noted, were viewed as synonymous with counterrevolutionaries, and the battle against nonconformity "was fought even in the area of sexual questions."

Pierre Herbart, who accompanied Gide on his trip, wrote in his diary that conversations everywhere in Moscow were "edifying and moral in nature." He said he was "so sick of virtue that I could throw up. I learned that boys no longer kiss girls without first having gone before the mayor; that homosexuals are mending their ways by reading Marx in concentration camps; that taxis must be lit up at night so as not to harbor sin; that the bedsheets of Red Army soldiers are inspected in order to shame those who masturbate; that children have no need for sex education because they never think about dirty things like that; that the fee for divorce is about to be raised, thereby putting it out of the reach of the poor; that it is unhealthy for people to enjoy themselves sexually without reproducing. This has all been proven by science, and everybody bows down in awe before its decrees."

The campaign against homosexuality in the Soviet Union served as a cutting edge in the efforts of Stalinism to secure a final stranglehold over the Soviet population in the mid-thirties—as antigay witch hunts have frequently aided the forces of reaction throughout history, and continue to do so today.

REGENERATION

The early homosexual rights movement was cut short, in the 1930s, after seventy years of existence, having achieved virtually no lasting breakthroughs. The small, isolated groups that came into existence here and there during the next two decades could not even be called holding actions, since there was little left to hold onto. The onslaught of Stalinism, fascism, and the ravages of World War II had wiped out virtually any trace of the first wave of gay liberation.

Today the gay liberation movement is in resurgence on an international scale never before seen. As it rediscovers and renews ties with its past, it will find not only inspiration in the first wave of gay assault on repressive morality and legality, but also important means for extending that struggle in the present and into the future.

ADDITIONAL NOTES ON FIVE PIONEERS

Karl Heinrich Ulrichs
(1825–1895)

In 1909, Magnus Hirschfeld wrote an article in which he pointed to Ulrichs as the great pioneer of the gay liberation struggle—despite the fact that his courageous and original work during the 1860s on behalf of gays had little impact at the time: "Should some future historian deal with the liberation struggle to which we have devoted our efforts, he will no doubt have to regard the activity of our Committee as the *second thrust* and assault against the unfortunate lack of understanding that has cost the lives and happiness of so many human beings. The *first assault* was made by Karl Heinrich Ulrichs during the sixties of the last century. In his numerous writings, he developed the most original ideas on the homosexual question, but his works did not achieve a very wide circulation, and his statements met with little response. His efforts to interest homosexuals themselves in the struggle for their liberation failed totally; as homosexuals saw the extent of the opposition their pioneers ran up against, they left him completely in the lurch."

In spite of this failure in the legal and political arena, however, Ulrichs' ideas did go on to be taken seriously by the medical establishment for years to come. After publishing his first two works, *Vindex* and *Inclusa*, under the pseudonym Numa Numantius, in 1864, Ulrichs went on during the next six years to publish nearly a dozen additional works under his own name.

Worn out by his single-handed struggle against formidable odds and opposition, Ulrichs then fled Germany—like so many others before him—to Italy, first to Naples, and then for more than twelve years, Aquila. There he passed his remaining days, in virtual oblivion, forgotten by his countrymen, and ignored, for the most part, by other gays.

One of the gays who did seek him out was John Addington Symonds. Symonds, who was then gathering material for his *Life of Michelangelo*, stayed with Ulrichs on October 27-28, 1891. In a letter written on October 29, 1891, from Rome, he described his meeting with Ulrichs:

"The main thing there [Aquila] was Ulrichs. J. spent a whole afternoon and evening in his company. Ulrichs is *Chrysostomos* [the meaning of which is "golden-mouthed"] to the last degree, sweet, noble, a true gentleman and man of genius. He must have been at one time a man of singular personal distinction, so finely cut are his features, and so grand the lines of his skull."

Ulrichs died at the age of seventy in 1895. As the gay movement that arose in the following years renewed ties with its past, his final resting place in Aquila appears to have taken on the character of a shrine. Hirschfeld, for instance, wrote of traveling there in April 1909 in terms suggesting the journey was for him a pilgrimage.

Magnus Hirschfeld
(1868–1935)

Hirschfeld was widely recognized in his day as a campaigner and educator in the field of sexology and homosexuality.

He was born in Kolberg, Germany, the son of a physician. Until 1887, he attended the Domgymnasium in his home town. In the early 1890s, he began his world travels, an occupation that was to be an important and regular part of his entire life. In 1893, he visited the World's Fair in Chicago, and then traveled throughout America, Africa, the Orient, and almost all the countries of Europe. Two years later, he settled in Charlottenburg, where he practiced medicine until 1909. He was a specialist in nervous and psychic maladies. From 1910 on, he practiced as a neurologist in Berlin.

Hirschfeld's life was devoted to spreading enlightenment about the nature of gays and others he considered "intermediate sexual types" (transvestites, hermaphrodites, etc.). This led him in 1897 to found the first gay organization, the Scientific Humanitarian Committee, and to be a regular contributor and guiding light to its Yearbook from

Magnus Hirschfeld

1899 until 1923. In 1896, he published his first book, *Sappho and Socrates*. By 1900, he was giving heavily attended lectures on "Love and Life" and "The Nature of the Human Personality."

In 1913, Hirschfeld joined Dr. Iwan Bloch and Dr. Heinrich Koerber to form the Medical Society for Sexual Science and Eugenics. In 1918, he founded the Magnus Hirschfeld Foundation for Sex Research, and in 1919, the Institute for Sexual Science. In 1921, he helped convene the first congress of the World League for Sexual Reform, an organization that was to continue its pioneering work in the area of sexual legislation and reform for more than a decade.

When the Nazis came to power, Hirschfeld was driven into exile both for being a sex reformer and a Jew. The Nazis called his work "undeutsch" (un-German), and actively sought to wipe out every trace of it. He died in France in 1935.

In its obituary on Hirschfeld, the *New York Herald Tribune* noted that "some fanciful writer once called Dr. Hirschfeld 'the Einstein of Sex,' because he adhered to the theory that sex endowments and impulses in the individual were 'relative.' There was no strict demarcation between the sexes, mentally or physically, he believed.

" 'Beneath the duality of sex there is a oneness,' he said. 'Every male is potentially a female and every female potentially a male. If a man wants to understand a woman, he must discover the woman in himself, and if a woman would understand a man, she must dig in her own consciousness to discover her own masculine traits.' "

Hirschfeld's methods of study, it explained, "were those of the consultant. He said once that he had talked with 30,000 men and women, who unburdened their troubles and maladjustments to him, confident that he could help them. Usually he could and did; each case that came to his institute received his personal attention. He devised a questionnaire which engaged persons might answer to determine before marriage if they were emotionally suited to each other. It was embarrassing, Dr. Hirschfeld used to say, how at parties, in private homes or public places, strangers to him, who knew his reputation as an emotional adjuster, would approach him and lay bare their souls.

"So this little, pudgy professor, with his Byronic neckties and his thick spectacles, who looked as if he never had got closer to human realities than drinking an occasional glass of beer, became a father confessor to thousands. He was a firm believer in the therapeutic value of full and frank verbal confession, like the psychiatrist and the parish priest, and he learned never to be surprised at what he heard. After hearing new and strange deviations from the norm, he began to wonder what the norm was and if there was such a Plimsoll mark of human nature."

Sir Richard Burton
(1821–1890)

The literary sensation of the year 1885 was the publication of the first ten volumes of the *Arabian Nights* (full title, *The Book of the Thousand Nights and a Night*), translated by Sir Richard Burton. Burton did not hold back when translating previously euphemized or omitted passages of erotica, but phrased them concretely and with gusto. Passages and whole sections dealing with pederasty, shunned by prior translators and editors, were translated fully, and homosexuality was treated as no less admirable than other forms of amorous expression. In addition, hundreds of footnotes, perhaps the most celebrated in English literature, displayed Burton's immense wealth of anthropological knowledge about sexual behavior.

At the end of the tenth volume came a "Terminal Essay," of which an 18,000 word section dealt with love between men and boys from an anthropological and historical standpoint. It was the first account of pederasty to appear openly in English, and the weightiest to appear in any language.

From the wealth of information contained in the "Terminal Essay" about how people in other cultures practiced and exalted homosexual love, an intelligent homosexual reader could easily construct a powerful defense of his own orientation. The essay, however, appears to be written on several levels and from a variety of contradictory viewpoints. In a single sentence, Burton extolled pederasty as "one of the marvellous list of amorous vagaries" and then apparently condemned it as "pathological love" which "deserved not prosecution but the pitiful care of the physician and the study of the psychologist."

Richard Burton on exploration in Africa, 1862.

The reason for such irreconcilable contradictions, running throughout the essay, is most likely due, not to schizophrenia on Burton's part, but to British censorship, which was far more severe than in the rest of Europe. Restrictions became tighter in the latter part of the Nineteenth Century. For example, in 1877, Charles Bradlaugh and Annie Besant were prosecuted for publishing a new edition of a pamphlet on birth control that had been freely sold in England for forty years. No doubt such trials were a warning to Burton. In 1888, the seventy-year-old publisher of an English translation of Zola's *La Terre* was fined and imprisoned for three months.

Burton's essay began by laying out a geographic theory about a "Sotadic Zone," approximately between latitudes 43' and 30', within which homosexuality flourished without social restraint. However, geographically the "Sotadic Zone" behaved rather strangely, undergoing extreme contractions and expansions; by the time the Sotadic Zone expanded to include the entire *hemisphere* of pre-Columbian America, it became a total *reductio ad absurdum* from the standpoint of geography. Clearly something more than geography was involved. Burton denied that the Sotadic Zone could be explained on racial grounds, and backed up his argument with evidence that within it all races practiced pederasty.

An astute reader might realize that the Sotadic Zone really conformed to the zone outside the repression of Christendom, for the evidence Burton presented established the boundaries of the Sotadic Zone as theological, not geographic—though Burton didn't say this directly—and much of the essay dealt in comparative religion. Burton demonstrated that historically the repression of homosexuality was a consequence of Judeo-Christian influence, and he contrasted the sensual freedom of other religions.

Burton referred to homosexuality as "vice," "Le Vice," "pathologic love," etc., throughout the essay. It is pretty clear, however, that he was writing tongue in cheek, for he also described pederasty with the warmest enthusiasm, and we know from biographical material that Burton began making love with boys in India when he was in his twenties, if not earlier. Thus the "Terminal Essay" was double-edged. The enlightened could read a powerful, well-documented defense of homosexual love, written with pride, relish, and even arrogance; while the pious could cluck their tongues disapprovingly over the "terrible vice."

The "Terminal Essay" concluded with a fierce attack on British censors. Burton's own attitude is probably expressed in two Latin phrases in the penultimate paragraph: "*Naturalia non sunt turpia*" ("Nature knows not corruption"or"There is no turpitude in the things of nature") and "*Mundis omnia munda*" ("To the pure, all things are pure").

Burton concluded his essay as follows: "It appears to me that when I show to such men [a critic Burton is lambasting], so 'respectable' and so impure, a landscape of magnificent prospects whose vistas are adorned with every charm of nature and art, they point their unclean noses at a little heap of muck here and there lying in a field corner."

The censors did not suppress *The Nights*, though a decade later they banned Havelock Ellis' *Studies in the Psychology of Sex* and more than four decades later, they banned the comparatively much tamer lesbian novel, *The Well of Loneliness*.

Burton's final project was a new translation of the erotic classic, *The Perfumed Garden*, which he had previously translated from a French translation. For his new work, to be called *The Scented Garden*, Burton went to the Arabic original, especially interested in translating the passages on pederasty; these had never before been rendered into a Western language. He intended to annotate it fully and to write a preface on homosexuality, incorporating the ideas of Ulrichs and others who had defended homosexual love. What had originally been a small book grew into a manuscript of more than 1,282 pages, and he told a friend, "I have put my whole life and all my life-blood into that *Scented Garden*; it is my great hope that I shall live by it. It is the crown of my life."

Burton and some friends had previously published six works of erotica, privately and in great secrecy. In a way, *The Scented Garden* was to be Burton's "coming out," the first step of which had been *The Nights* and the "Terminal Essay."

The day before he was to put the finishing touches on his manuscript, Burton died, at the age of sixty-nine. Had he lived only a few days longer, England and the world might have seen a fighting polemic for homosexual freedom. But Burton's wife, a fanatical Roman Catholic, burned the manuscript of *The Scented Garden*, and also destroyed the personal journals Burton had faithfully kept every day for over forty years.

Burton, who had loathed Christianity, was given *two* Roman Catholic funerals by Isabel. The second, held in London eight months after his death, was boycotted by most of his friends, who were incensed by the vulgar and superstitious disregard of everything Burton, the rebel and pagan, had stood for.

Swinburne wrote:

> *Priests and the soulless serfs of priests may swarm*
> *With vulturous acclamation, loud in lies,*
> *About his dust while yet his dust is warm*
> *Who mocked as sunlight mocks their base blind eyes.*
>
> *Their godless ghost of godhead, false and foul*
> *As fear his dam or hell his throne: but we*
> *Scarce hearing, heed no carrion church-kites howl:*
> *The corpse be theirs to mock; the soul is free.*

Sir Richard Burton was the foremost orientalist of his age. He spoke twenty-five languages—with dialects included, a total of forty languages. He had learned classical Latin at the age of three, and classical Greek at four. He was one of the greatest British explorers of the Nineteenth Century. Burton was the author of more than fifty books; his translation of the *Arabian Nights* is one of the treasures of the English language. He was also considered to be the foremost swordsman of his time. Finally, he was an outstanding early anthropologist.

Walt Whitman
(1819-1892)

In his *Leaves of Grass*, especially its "Calamus" section (1860), Whitman celebrated passionate friendship between males (which he called "manly love") in which unabashed physical contact played an

Walt Whitman in 1883.

important part. His songs in praise of homosexual love stirred European gays, who saw in him a kind of prophet. Not only were his works avidly read, but the nature of his homosexuality itself became a topic of conversation for decades at a time when gays were looking for prominent figures to speak for them to a public ignorant of their needs and love. And Whitman's exuberant celebration of gay love was a breath of fresh air, especially in England, smothered under the restraints and prudish conventions of the Victorian era.

It was this side of Whitman that prompted John Addington Symonds to write to him, openly raising the issue of his homosexuality. But by the time Whitman answered the query in August 19, 1890, he was apparently attempting to convey the impression that he was not really gay and that he regarded such inquiries as an intrusion. He had, for instance, engaged in "drag writing" by changing one of his poems ("I passed through a populous city"), straightening it out by substituting a woman for a man. Whitman wrote to Symonds:

"About the questions on 'Calamus,' etc., they quite daze me. *Leaves of Grass* is only to be rightly construed by and within its own atmosphere and essential character—all its pages and pieces so coming strictly under. That the 'Calamus' part has ever allowed the possibility of such construction as mentioned is terrible. I am fain to hope that the pages themselves are not to be even mentioned for such gratuitous and quite at the time undreamed and unwished possibility of morbid inferences—which are disavowed by me and seem damnable."

Whitman's disclaimers were not taken seriously by those of his friends and acquaintances who knew better. "It would seem from this letter," wrote Havelock Ellis in his *Studies in the Psychology of Sex*, "that Whitman had never realized that there is any relationship whatever between the passionate emotion of physical contact from man to man, as he had experienced it and sung it, and the act which with other people he would regard as a crime against nature. This may be singular, for there are many inverted persons who have found satisfaction in friendships less physical and passionate than those described in *Leaves of Grass*, but Whitman was a man of concrete, emotional, instinctive temperament, lacking in analytical power, receptive to all influences, and careless of harmonizing them. He would most certainly have refused to admit that he was the subject of inverted sexuality. It remains true, however, that 'manly love' occupies in his work a predominance which it would scarcely hold in the feelings of the 'average man,' whom Whitman wishes to honor."

And in 1924, Edward Carpenter wrote: "He, Whitman, could hardly with truthfulness deny any knowledge or contemplation of such inferences; but if on the other hand he took what we might call the reasonable line, and said that, while not *advocating* abnormal relations in any way, he of course made allowance for possibilities in that direction and the occasional development of such relations, why, he knew that the moment he said such a thing he would have the whole American Press at his heels, snarling and slandering, and distorting his words in every possible way. Things are pretty bad here in this country, but in the States (in such matters) they are ten times worse."

Despite Whitman's refusals to publicly champion the homosexual cause, his work must be regarded as a courageous and inspiring contribution to the growing awareness of gay pride among homosexuals during the second half of the Nineteenth Century.

Edward Carpenter
(1844-1929)

In his autobiography, *My Days and Dreams*, Carpenter noted that Walt Whitman, "the poet who was destined so deeply to influence my life," was the first poet he had read to treat sex in a way that "accorded with my own sentiments." He first read Whitman in the late 1860s. He was mesmerized: "I had never found anything approaching these writings of Whitman's for their inexhaustible quality and power of making one return to them." His newfound passion for Whitman coincided more or less with a growing distaste for the religious vocation (that of a priest in the Church of England) into which he had been ordained, virtually in spite of himself; he did not agree with the church's doctrines, and said so at the time.

It also occurred at a historical conjuncture that was giving rise to a new movement of women, dissatisfied with the hopelessness of their

Edward Carpenter in 1910.

lives under an advancing process of industrialization that offered them not emancipation but increased subjugation and exploitation.

Whitman, with his forthright praise of homosexual love, and the women's movement, with its militant challenging of traditional sex roles and institutionalized oppression, were to remain fundamental inspirations to Carpenter throughout his life. He went on in his work to apply that inspiration to the cause of homosexual liberation.

"The Uranian temperament in Man," he wrote, "closely resembles the normal temperament of Woman in this respect, that in both, Love—in some form or other—is the main object of life. In the normal Man, ambition, moneymaking, business, adventure, etc., play their part—Love is as a rule a secondary matter. The majority of men (for whom the physical side of sex, if needed, is easily accessible) do not for a moment realize the griefs endured by thousands of girls and women—in the drying up of a wellspring of affection as well as in the crucifixion of their physical needs. But as these sufferings of women, of one kind or another, have been the great inspiring cause and impetus of the Women's Movement—a movement which is already having a great influence in the reorganization of society; so I do not practically doubt that the similar sufferings of the Uranian class of men are destined in their turn to lead to another wide-reaching social organization and forward movement in the direction of Art and Human Compassion."

Carpenter viewed the present stage of social evolution, which he termed "civilisation," as a "somewhat peculiar state of society" that "even to the most optimistic among us does not seem altogether desirable." He was inclined to think, he wrote in *Civilisation: Its Cause and Cure*, that it was a "kind of disease which the various races of man have to pass through—as children pass through measles or whooping cough. . . ."

To him, the Victorian Age was "the lowest ebb of modern civilised society: a period in which not only commercialism in public life, but cant in religion, pure materialism in science, futility in social conventions, the worship of stocks and shares, the starving of the human heart, the denial of the human body and its needs, the huddling concealment of the body in clothes, the 'impure hush' on matters of sex, class-division, contempt of manual labour, and the cruel barring of women from every natural and useful expression of their lives, were carried to an extremity of folly difficult for us now to realize."

Carpenter had a vision of a revolution destroying the existing "commercial regime" and bringing about a new society where human beings could rediscover (on a higher level) the lost freedom of the past (including the freedom to love members of the same sex). Describing this vision in his autobiography, he wrote: "With that transformation of industry all life will be transformed, and the neo-Pagan ideal will become a thing possible of realization." The new society "shall embody to the fullest extent the two opposite poles of Communism and Individualism in one vital unity."

It was this vision that attracted Carpenter to the socialist movement of his day in the early 1880s. "The real value of the modern Socialist movement—it has always seemed to me—has not lain so much in its actual constructive programme as (1) in the fact that it has provided a text for a searching criticism of the old society and of the lives of the rich, and (2) the fact that it has enshrined a most glowing and vital enthusiasm towards the realization of a new society." Carpenter, a kind of counterculturalist, saw the socialist movement less in terms of its theoretical contributions, or even of strategy, than as a convenient and effective tool for combatting the injustices of capitalism.

Uranians, who, he felt, combined qualities of both sexes, were destined to become "to a large extent the teachers of future society" in "affairs of the heart." In *The Intermediate Sex*, he wrote: ". . . it is possible that the Uranian spirit may lead to something like a general enthusiasm of Humanity, and that the Uranian people may be destined to form the advance guard of that great movement which will one day transform the common life by substituting the bond of personal affection and compassion for the monetary, legal and other external ties which now control and confine society. Such a part of course we cannot expect the Uranians to play unless the capacity for their kind of attachment also exists—though in a germinal and undeveloped state—in the breast of mankind at large. And modern thought and investigation are clearly tending that way—to confirm that it does so exist."

Carpenter felt that a potential for homosexuality existed in everybody. In this, he was closer to Benedict Friedländer than those who, like Hirschfeld, reduced sexual behavior to little more than a rigid reflection of biology and physiology.

Carpenter went so far as to suggest that gays were superior to straights. "Unwilling as the world at large is to credit what I am about to say," he wrote, "and great as are the current misunderstandings on the subject, I believe it is true that the Uranian men are superior to the normal men in this respect—in respect of their love-feeling—which is gentler, more sympathetic, more considerate, more a matter of the heart and less one of mere physical satisfaction than that of ordinary men."

The following poems are reprinted from *Towards Democracy*, by Edward Carpenter.

As a Woman of a Man

Democracy!
O sombre swart face, now thou art very beau-
tiful to me!
O haughty brow, with glittering withdrawn eyes, not a
little contemptuous,
Thou art very beautiful to me!

I am as a child before thee;
All that I have learned, all my fancical knowledge,
My familiarity with times and distances,
All my refinement is nothing—my delicate hands,
manners,
My glibness is nothing;
I crave the touch of thy soul, thou strong one,
I crave thy love.

Come! who art no longer a name:
Gigantic Thou, with head aureoled by the sun—wild
among the mountains—
Thy huge limbs naked and stalwart erected member,
Thy lawless gait and rank untameable laughter,
Thy heaven-licking wildfire thoughts and passions—
I desire.

All conventions, luxuries, all refinements of civilization,
and tyrannous wants,
Acquisitions, formulated rules, rights, prescriptions, and
whatever constitutes a barrier—
I discard.

All the cobwebs of science, and precedents and con-
clusions of authority,
All possessions, and impedimenta of property, all rights
of bundles and baggage—
I disown.

I stand prepared for toil, for hardship—this instant if
need be to start on an unforeseen and distant journey—
I am wholly without reserve:
As a woman of a man so I will learn of thee,
I will draw thee closer and closer,
I will drain thy lips and the secret things of thy body,
I will conceive by thee, Democracy.

These Populations

These populations—
So puny, white-faced, machine made,
Turned out of factories, out of offices, out of
drawing-rooms, by thousands all alike—
Huddled, stitched up, in clothes, fearing a chill, a drop of
rain, looking timidly at the sea and sky as at strange

monsters, or running back so quick to their suburban runs and burrows,

Dapper, libidinous, cute, with washed-out small eyes—
What are these?
Are they men and women?
Each denying himself, hiding himself?
Are they men and women?
So timorous, like hares—a breath of propriety or custom, a draught of wind, the mere threat of pain or of danger?

O for a breath of the sea and the great mountains!
A bronzed hardy live man walking his way through it all;
Thousands of men companioning the waves and the storms, splendid in health, naked-breasted, catching the lion with their hands;
A thousand women swift-footed and free—owners of themselves, forgetful of themselves, in all their actions—full of joy and laughter and action;
Garbed not so differently from the men, joining with them in their games and sports, sharing also their labors;
Free to hold their own, to grant or withhold their love, the same as the men;
Strong, well-equipped in muscle and skill, clear of finesse and affectation—
(The men, too, clear of much brutality and conceit)—
Comrades together, equal in intelligence and adventure,
Trusting without concealment, loving without shame but with discrimination and continence towards a perfect passion.

O for a breath of the sea!
The necessity and directness of the great elements themselves!
Swimming the rivers, braving the sun, the cold, taming the animals and the earth, conquering the air with wings, and each other with love—
The true the human society!

Source Bibliography

Allworth, Edward (Editor). *Soviet Nationality Problems*. New York and London: Columbia University Press, 1971.

Batkis, Grigorii. *Die Sexualrevolution in Russland*. Berlin: Fritz Kater, 1925.

Bernstein, Eduard. *Die Neue Zeit*. #32 (April 26, 1895), "Aus Anlass eines Sensationsprozess"; #34 (May 6, 1895) "Beurtheilung des widernormalen Geschlechtsverkehrs."

Bol'shaîa Sovetskaîa Entsiklopedîa (Great Soviet Encyclopedia). Moscow: First Edition (1930), Third Edition (1971), *s.v. gomoseksualizm*.

Brand, Adolf. *Paragraph 175*, Berlin-Wilhelmshagen: Der Eigene, 1914.

British Society for the Study of Sex Psychology. "The Problem of Sexual Inversion." London, 1923.

Brodie, Fawn M. *The Devil Drives: A Life of Sir Richard Burton*. New York: W.W. Norton & Company, 1967.

Carpenter, Edward. *Civilisation: Its Cause and Cure*. London: Swan Sonnenschein & Co., 1889.

_____ *The Intermediate Sex*. New York and London: Mitchell Kennerley, 1912.

_____ *Love's Coming-of-Age*. New York and London: Mitchell Kennerley, 1912.

_____ *My Days and Dreams*. New York: Charles Scribner's Sons, 1916.

_____ *Some Friends of Walt Whitman: A Study in Sex Psychology*. Published by the British Society for the Study of Sex Psychology, 1924.

_____ *Towards Democracy*. New York and London: Mitchell Kennerley, 1912.

Daniels, Robert V. (Editor). *A Documentary History of Communism From Lenin to Mao*. New York: Random House, 1960.

Dearden, Seton. *Burton of Arabia*. New York: National Travel Club, 1937.

Ellis, Havelock. *Studies in the Psychology of Sex*. New York: Random House, 1942.

Ellmann, Richard (Editor). *Oscar Wilde: A Collection of Critical Essays*. New Jersey: Prentice-Hall, 1969.

Friedländer, Benedict. *Die Liebe Platons im Lichte der modernen Biologie*. Treptow bei Berlin: Bernhard Zack, 1909.

_____ *Renaissance des Eros Uranios*. Berlin: Otto Lehmann, 1904.

Gide, André. *Retour de l'U.R.S.S.* Paris: Gallimard, 1936.

Guérin, Daniel. *Fascism and Big Business*. New York: Monad Press, 1973.

Henault, Mirta. "La Mujer y los Cambios Sociales," in las Mujeres Dicen BASTA. Buenos Aires: Ediciones Nueva Mujer, 1973.

Herbart, Pierre. *En U.R.S.S.* Paris: Gallimard, 1936.

Hiller, Kurt. *Leben gegen die Zeit*, vol. 2 [*Eros*], Hamburg: Rowohlt, 1973.

_____ "Appeal to the Second International Congress for Sexual Reform on the Behalf of an Oppressed Variety of Human Being," translated by John

Lauritsen. New York: The Red Butterfly, 1970.

Him, "Als Homohass die Welt in Flammen setzte: Die Geschichte des 30. Juni (IV)." January 1973, p. 35.

Hirschfeld, Magnus. *Berlins drittes Geschlecht.* Berlin and Leipzig: Verlag Hermann Seemann, 1904.

_____ *Geschlecht und Verbrechen.* Leipzig and Vienna: Verlag für Sexualwissenschaft, Schneider & Co., 1930.

_____ *Sex in Human Relationships* (Introduction by Norman Haire). London and Redhill: Athenaeum, 1935.

_____ *Sexual Anomalies.* New York: Random House, 1942.

_____ *Die Weltreise eines Sexualforschers.* Brugg: Bözberg Verlag, 1933.

Hyde, H. Montgomery. *The Love That Dared Not Speak Its Name.* Boston and Toronto: Little, Brown and Company, 1970.

_____ *Oscar Wilde: The Aftermath.* New York: Farrar, Straus & Company, 1963.

_____ *The Three Trials of Oscar Wilde.* New York: University Books, 1956.

Jahrbuch für sexuelle Zwischenstufen. Leipzig: Max Spohr.

Joll, James. *The Second International.* London: Weidenfeld & Nicolson, 1955.

Krafft-Ebing, Richard von. *Psychopathia Sexualis.* New York: Pioneer Publications, 1943.

Kuzmin, Mikhail. *Wings: Prose and Poetry by Mikhail Kuzmin.* Ann Arbor: Ardis Publishers, 1972.

_____ *Zanaveshannye Kartinki.* Amsterdam (Petrograd), 1920. (Facsimile edition by Ardis Publishers, 1972).

Landauer, Carl A. *European Socialism.* Berkeley and Los Angeles: University of California Press, 1959.

Mayne, Xavier. *The Intersexes: A History of Similisexualism as a Problem in Social Life.* Privately printed in Italy, 1908.

Mother Earth. Emma Goldman, Publisher. New York.

Pearson, Hesketh. *The Life of Oscar Wilde.* London: Methuen & Co., 1954.

Reade, Brian (Editor). *Sexual Heretics.* New York: Coward-McCann, Inc. 1971.

Reich, Ilse Ollendorff. *Wilhelm Reich: A Personal Biography.* New York: St. Martin's Press, 1969.

Reich, Wilhelm. *The Mass Psychology of Fascism.* New York: Farrar, Straus & Giroux, 1970.

_____ *The Sexual Revolution.* New York: Farrar, Straus & Giroux, 1970.

Steakley, Jim. *Body Politic.* Series on the gay movement in Germany. Numbers 9, 10, and 11. Toronto.

Trotsky, Leon. *Literature and Revolution.* New York: Russell & Russell.

_____ *The Revolution Betrayed.* New York: Pioneer Publishers, 1945.

Whitman, Walt. *Poems of Walt Whitman.* New York: Thomas Y. Crowell & Company, 1902.

Wilde, Oscar. *Collected Works* (with introduction by Vyvyan Holland). London: Methuen & Co., 1954.

World League for Sexual Reform. (Proceedings of Congresses) Berlin, 1921; Copenhagen, 1928; London, 1929; Vienna, 1930.

INDEX

Action Committee, 16, 30-31
Andreas-Salomé, Lou, 14
Argentina, 25
Austria, 30, 31, 38, 39, 44, 57, 66, 67
Ballad of Reading Gaol, The (Wilde), 57-58
Bang, Herman, 25
Batkis, Grigorii, 4, 63-64, 90
Bebel, August, 13-14, 27, 60
Belgium, 31
Benkert, Karoly Maria, 6-8, 9
Bernstein, Eduard, 14, 58-59, 90
bisexuality, 50-51
Bjoernson, Bjoernstjerne, 14, 15
Bloch, Iwan, 75
Bolshevism, 62-67
Brand, Adolf, 19-21, 67, 90
Brandes, Georg, 14
Braunschweig, Rosa von, 17
Brazil, 25
Brod, Max, 14
Brown Book of The Hitler Terror, The, 40-41
Buber, Martin, 14
Bulgaria, 34
Bülow, Bernhard von, 21
Burchard, Ernst, 10
Burton, Sir Richard, 51, 76-80
Canada, 36
Carpenter, Edward, 32-34, 37, 41, 83-89, 90
China, 40
Civilisation: Its Causes and Cures (Carpenter), 85
Community of the Special, 13, 16, 19, 30
Cuba, 67
Czechoslovakia, 30, 39, 66
Denmark, 12, 25, 31, 39, 66
"Different from Other People" (motion picture), 25, 28-29
Einstein, Albert, 14
Ellis, Havelock, 34, 37, 41, 51, 79, 82, 90
Engels, Friedrich, 27
England, 9, 26, 30, 31-35, 41, 51, 52-59, 66, 67, 76, 77-80, 82, 83, 85-87
Eros Theater (Berlin), 30
Eulenburg, Philipp zu, 19-21
France, 6, 12, 41, 43, 56, 67, 75
Freud, Sigmund, 19, 41, 47, 64
Friedländer, Benedict, 19-21, 50-51, 87, 90

Gens, A., 67
German Friendship Association, 13, 16
German Women's Congress (1912), 34
Germany, 6-31, 34, 36, 39, 40-45, 52, 57, 58-62, 66, 67-68, 69, 72, 73-76
Gide, André, 41, 70, 90
Goldman, Emma, 36-37, 91
Gorki, Maxim, 69
Great Soviet Encyclopedia, 64-65, 90
Grosz, George, 14
Haire, Norman, 41, 45
Hall, Radclyffe, 35, 79
Harden, Maximilian, 19-21
Harris, Frank, 57
Hauptmann, Gerhart, 14
Herbart, Pierre, 70, 90
Hesse, Hermann, 14
Hilferding, Rudolf, 14
Hiller, Kurt, 16, 38, 43, 90
Hirschfeld, Magnus, 9-11, 14, 15, 16, 18, 19, 23-25, 26, 29, 30, 36, 37, 38, 39-40, 41-42, 47-51, 56, 57, 60, 64, 65, 72-76, 87, 91
Holland, 12, 30, 31, 34, 37-38, 65
Institute for Sexual Science (Berlin), 27-29, 40-43, 75
Intermediate Sex, The (Carpenter), 86
International Medical Congress (1913), 29, 41
Intersexes, The (Stevenson), 36
Italy, 30, 31, 34, 36, 39, 72-73
Japan, 34
Jaurès, Jean Léon, 27
Kautsky, Karl, 14
Koerber, Heinrich, 75
Kollwitz, Käthe, 14
Krafft-Ebing, Richard von, 14, 36, 37, 39, 47, 59, 91
Kuzmin, Mikhail, 65, 66, 91
Lassalle, Ferdinand, 27, 52
League for the Protection of Mothers, 15
Leaves of Grass (Whitman), 32, 80, 82
Lesbians, 17-18
Leunbach, J. H., 41, 45
Liebknecht, Wilhelm, 27
Linsert, Richard, 68
Loti, Pierre, 41
Love's Coming-of-Age (Carpenter), 33
Mann, Heinrich, 14
Mann, Thomas, 14

Books from Times Change Press

JANUARY THAW: People at Blue Mt. Ranch Write About Living Together in the Mountains. Writing about relationships, work, parents, children, healing and celebration, these rural communards describe feeling their way toward a life that makes sense and feels good, in which people are more in harmony with themselves, each other, the earth and the universe. *Illustrated; 160 pp; $3.25. Cloth, $8.50.*

THE EARLY HOMOSEXUAL RIGHTS MOVEMENT (1864-1935)—John Lauritsen and David Thorstad. The gay movement, like the women's movement, has an early history, which, beginning in 1864, advanced the cause of gay rights until the 1930s when Stalinist and Nazi repression obliterated virtually all traces of it. The authors uncover this history, highlighting interesting people and events. *Illustrated; 96 pp; $2.25. Cloth, $6.95.*

MOMMA: A Start on All the Untold Stories—Alta. This is Alta's intensely personal story of her life with her two young daughters, and her struggle to be a writer. She tells of her efforts toward self-fulfillment and her battle against feelings of guilt—a story many readers will recognize as their own. *Illustrated; 80 pp; $2.00. Cloth, $6.50.*

AMAZON EXPEDITION: A Lesbianfeminist Anthology—Edited by Phyllis Birkby, Bertha Harris, Jill Johnston, Esther Newton and Jane O'Wyatt. When lesbians within the gay liberation movement synthesized gay politics with feminism, they started a separate political/cultural development which thousands of women began to identify with. This is what this anthology is about. Culture, herstory, politics, celebration. Lesbianfeminism—one concept: the new womanity. *Illustrated; 96 pp; $2.25. Cloth, $6.50.*

LISTEN TO THE MOCKING BIRD: Satiric Songs To Tunes You Know—Tuli Kupferberg. Radical songs can't make the new world, but they can help. And they can help you endure this one. Especially if they're humorous. Over 50 songs to delight and thrill you and yes make you laugh. *Illustrated; 64 pp; $1.50.*

THIS WOMAN: Poetry of Love and Change—Barbara O'Mary. This journal tells of a year of intense change—involving Barbara's lovers male and female, her daughters, her job, her politics, her fears, her visions. Simple, intimate and honest poetry which we identify with immediately, as it clarifies our own experience. *Illustrated; 64 pp; $1.50.*

LESSONS FROM THE DAMNED: Class Struggle in the Black Community—By The Damned. This book describes the awareness of oppression as black people, as workers and poor people under capitalism, and as women and young people oppressed by men and the family. It may be the first time that poor and petit-bourgeois black people have told their own story. *Illustrated; 160 pp; $2.75. Cloth, $7.95.*

SOME PICTURES FROM MY LIFE: A Diary—Marcia Salo Rizzi. Marcia has selected entries from her diary and combined them with her emotionally powerful ink-brush drawings—one woman's experience reflecting pictures from the lives of all women. *Illustrated; 64 pp; $1.35.*

GREAT GAY IN THE MORNING!: One Group's Approach to Communal Living and Sexual Politics—The 25 to 6 Baking & Trucking Society. These are personal accounts of seven gay men and two lesbians writing about their experiences in over three years of communal living, gay consciousness-raising, and political involvement. *Illustrated; 96 pp; $2.25. Cloth, $4.95.*

BEGIN AT START: Some Thoughts on Personal Liberation and World Change—Su Negrin. A Times Change Press editor writes about her experiences in various liberation movements (mysticism, free school, commune, new left, feminist and gay) and talks about how they're all coming together in a new way—transforming individuals and approaching a utopia more awesome than we have ever dreamed of. *Illustrated; 176 pp; $2.75. Cloth, $6.95.*

YOUTH LIBERATION: News, Politics and Survival Information—Youth Liberation of Ann Arbor. The authors write about the oppression of being young in an adult chauvinist society—imprisonment in families and schools, economic dependence, denial of legal rights—and they describe the growing activity toward world-wide youth liberation. *Illustrated; 64 pp; $1.75.*

FREE OURSELVES: Forgotten Goals of the Revolution—Arthur Aron; Illustrations by Elaine N. Blesi. In our movement for social change, we have in many ways, lost touch with our humanistic values. Art believes that to realize our values we must *live* them—now—by changing ourselves and creating a giant personal/social/cultural alternative. *Illustrated; 64 pp; $1.35.*

WOODHULL AND CLAFLIN'S WEEKLY: The Lives and Writings of Victoria Woodhull and Tennessee Claflin—Arlene Kisner, Editor/Biographer. Throughout their notorious careers, Victoria and Tennie were involved in the radical developments of their time—socialism, mysticism, women's rights. These selections from their (in)famous newsmagazine (1870-1876) are interspersed with Arlene's detailed biographical sketches. *Illustrated; 64 pp; $1.35.*

UNBECOMING MEN: A Men's Consciousness-Raising Group Writes on Oppression and Themselves. This book reflects the struggles of a group of men who've come together because of their increasingly unavoidable awareness of sexism—how it operates against the people they most care for and ultimately, how it eats away at their own humanity. *Illustrated; 64 pp; $1.75.*

GENERATIONS OF DENIAL: 75 Short Biographies of Women in History—Kathryn Taylor. These women were whole people under the worst of circumstances, worse still for those who, in addition to being female, were gay. These biographies are a pioneering collection with which to supplement history books and women's pride. *Illustrated; 64 pp; $1.35.*

BURN THIS AND MEMORIZE YOURSELF: Poems for Women—Alta; Photographs by Ellen Shumsky. An unusual pamphlet of plain-talking poems, set against a background of photographs, showing women in many of the new ways they are beginning to be together—self-sufficient, intimate, loving, self-defined. *Illustrated; 16 pp; 50¢.*

FREE SPACE: A Perspective on the Small Group in Women's Liberation—Pamela Allen. *Free Space* is a good handbook for people wondering how to begin or restructure a consciousness-raising group. Developed by feminists, the small group is now being used by many people as a way of relating to different needs. *Illustrated; 64 pp; $1.75.*

ECOLOGY AND REVOLUTIONARY THOUGHT—Murray Bookchin. This book widens the scope of the ecological problem by asserting that people's domination over nature is rooted in our domination over each other. Murray takes into account the social/political crises that are inseparable from our environmental one. *Illustrated; 64 pp; $1.25.*

THE TRAFFIC IN WOMEN and Other Essays on Feminism—Emma Goldman; with a biography by Alix Kates Shulman. Emma Goldman was a dynamic anarchist and so her feminism differed markedly from her suffrage-oriented contemporaries. Today the split between liberal and radical approaches to women's liberation are still not resolved. So these essays have an uncanny relevancy to problems now being dealt with. *Illustrated; 64 pp; $1.35.*

WITH LOVE, SIRI AND EBBA—Siri Fraser and Ebba Pedersen. Siri and Ebba are two young women who decided to hitch-hike through northern Africa to Sudan and Ethiopia. These letters, drawings and photographs tell the story of their adventure and of their love for "the most fantastic free wild nomadic tribes" people, with whom they lived. *Illustrated; 128 pp; $3.25. Cloth, $8.50.*
